Freelance Writing For Hollywood
How to Pitch, Write and Sell Your Work

Scott Essman

"Scott is everything in one: a wonderful writer, editor, listener and effective communicator. I learn something new from him every time he helps me with my writing; his ability to collaborate is brilliant. For over two years now, I've been calling Scott — he's the best writing mentor I could ask for."

Deborah Lynn, Entertainment Industry Executive Assistant

"In 1996, after establishing myself as a makeup/creature artist, Scott was able to produce a half-hour documentary about my children's film project, *Wolvy*. That video is now part of my selling package for the project, and since that time, Scott and I have become friends and continued to work together. The door will always be open for him to professionally cover my projects."

Todd Tucker, Producer of Wonderworld Entertainment

"I have always thought that makeup artistry was one of the oddest professions, but Scott Essman's marvelous book **Freelance Writing for Hollywood** reveals and explains the challenges and how-to's of his equally unusual profession."

Dick Smith, Academy Award-Winning Makeup Artist and Pioneer

FREELANCE WRITING FOR HOLLYWOOD

HOW TO PITCH, WRITE AND SELL YOUR WORK

SCOTT ESSMAN

Published by Michael Wiese Productions, 11288 Ventura Blvd., Suite 821, Studio City, CA
91604, (818) 379-8799 Fax (818) 986-3408.
E-mail: mw@mwp.com
www.mwp.com

Cover design, The Art Hotel
Interior design and layout, Gina Mansfield
Editor, Carsten Dau

Printed by McNaughton & Gunn, Inc., Saline, Michigan
Manufactured in the United States of America

Library of Congress Cataloging-in-Publication Data

Essman, Scott.
    Freelance Writing for Hollywood : how to pitch, write and sell your work / Scott
Essman.
      p. cm.
    ISBN 0-941188-27-2
    1. Motion picture authorship. I. Title

PN 1996 .E85 2000
808.2'3--dc21

                                                                00-033362

Dedication

To my aunt, Alice Essman-Schwartz (1949-1997), who always
believed in what I was doing, even before there was any concrete
evidence of success.

FREELANCE WRITING FOR HOLLYWOOD
HOW TO PITCH, WRITE AND SELL YOUR WORK
BY SCOTT ESSMAN

TABLE OF CONTENTS

ACKNOWLEDGEMENTS

It goes without saying that a freelance writer's career is impossible to create without the support of many passionate individuals; as such, this book represents the fulfillment of my relationships with many of those folks. First and foremost, I must thank the many makeup artists and fans whose creative work originally inspired me to enter their world – an especially fond thanks to Tom and Bari Burman, who granted me my first interview in that field. Also, heartfelt thanks to Dick Smith and John Chambers, each legendary artists who were the subjects of my first two tributes—I am proud to now call them both friends and collaborators. Equal in their contributions to my projects were Brian Penikas and his "Apemania" team; Bill Corso, Kenny and Karen Myers at Cinémakeup Studios, and the entire *Wizard of Oz* dream team of artists and performers; Jennifer McManus and Rob Burman of Sticks and Stones, who hung in there with me for over a year while planning the Jack Pierce tribute, and kindred spirit Todd Tucker of Wonderworld Entertainment. Finally, many thanks go out to the valiant coordinators, assistants and intake personnel at the various production and publicity offices, studios, record companies and magazines, all of whom not only helped to make my job (and life) easier, but many of whom actually contributed to my work in a positive manner. Among these extra special troopers are Howard Green, Zelda Wong, and Jeff Hare at Disney; John Landis and staff at St. Clare Entertainment; Michael Key and staff of Makeup Artist Magazine; Tim Rhys and the invaluable Emily Farbman at MovieMaker; Alain Schlockoff at L'Ecran Fantastique; Erik Bauer at Creative Screenwriting; Enrique Diaz at *Nuvein Online*; Don and Estelle Shay at Cinefex; and A+ publicists including BeBe Lerner, Rhonda Stein, Gihan Salem, Nicole Ross, Kristin Borella, Anne Reilly at HBO in LA, Tobe Becker at HBO in New York, and the greatest publicist in the world, Jeanmarie Murphy-Burke, who strives to make writers' lives better all the time. Sincere apologies to those specific colleagues who I may have omitted, but if you were integral to the process, you know who you are! Thanks for the support, and here's looking forward to future collaborations.

Finally, an extra special thanks to those friends and family who have been supportive, to Carsten Dau for his integral editorial contributions, and to Dr. Laurel Jones for her eleventh hour input. A big thumbs up, folks.

Arthur William Edgar O'Shaughnessy
1844-1881

Ode

We are the music-makers,
And we are the dreamers of dreams,
Wandering by lone sea breakers,
And sitting by desolate streams;
World-losers and world-forsakers,
On whom the pale moon gleams:
Yet we are the movers and shakers
Of the world forever, it seems.

INTRODUCTION

At 9:00 on Halloween morning, 1998, Hollywood Boulevard was lined with 3,000 parents, children, and Warner Bros. media representatives, all waiting, ostensibly, for a very special surprise. I was responsible for producing a portion of the day's proceedings, but I was shamefully naive about what I was about to instigate. Much like Brian Epstein must have felt when viewing the hordes of teenagers as the Beatles arrived at Kennedy airport in New York back in 1964, I wondered why the crowds had gathered three hours prior to this scheduled noon event, a special screening of the re-furbished film classic *The Wizard of Oz*. Then it dawned on me: those kids dressed in various *Oz* incarnations and their doting parents were waiting there for a personal appearance from some of cinema's most beloved characters, mainly, the five performers who were accompanying me in the Warner Bros. limousine and who had been made-up and costumed as exact recreations of Dorothy, the Scarecrow, the Tin Man, the Lion, and the Wicked Witch from the 1939 MGM classic. And feeling the same way Epstein

must have felt when he contemplated entering a sea of Beatlemaniacs, I began to determine how to navigate my people through the somewhat more subdued throng of *Oz* devotees. With awe and apprehension, I escorted the characters out of the limo through the hand-printed courtyard of Mann's Chinese Theater, up a makeshift yellow brick road. The huge crowd's overwhelming reaction to the characters was unforgettable. It was straight out of the movies.

"How did I ever get to this point?" I thought, watching the crowds erupt into a combination of laughter, cheers, and surprise. The answer to that question eventually became the foundation for this volume, and the journey that I took to get this Yellow Brick Road is one that I share openly with other would-be freelance writers eager to enter their own Emerald City, particularly the one in Hollywood. It must be said that my journey was consciously designed to be an unprecedented one, and perhaps, in light of that fact, it cannot be specifically replicated by others (or by me, for that matter!) in either its methodology or focus. Yet if any writer wishes to forge his or her own path towards the same goal — a self-made career in entertainment journalism and production, I offer one person's experience and my sincerest wishes for achieving your own version of success in the quest. Plus, as I will underscore in coming chapters, one should never take any form of information for granted; even if you only take note of small bits and pieces of the advice and anecdotes here - even those that seemingly have no immediate consequence - you can never tell when information will prove to be incalculably valuable.

My offbeat journey has taken me into the domain of the geniuses behind several defining moments from 20th century cinema culture. Before their respective anniversaries were even recognized by the mainstream media, I translated my childhood love for films such as *Planet of the Apes*, *The Wizard of Oz*, and the Universal horror classics into unprecedented multi-media events, each of which led to a flurry of news articles, magazine assignments, international video sales, and ultimately, book contracts. Strategically, I maneuvered myself into the right time and place to write about *The Matrix* before it became a hit, about *Star Wars* before it was hip again, and about *Willy Wonka and the Chocolate Factory*, which, as of this printing, has yet to be resurrected into popular consciousness for its 30th anniversary. And, through a specific plan and purpose, I found myself invited onto George Lucas' Skywalker Ranch, the backlot of Universal Studios, and the famed soundstages at Warner Bros., Disney and Paramount, not as a tourist, but as a professional writer conducting business. By personal choice, I researched and wrote about such personal favorites as *Raging Bull*, *2001: A Space Odyssey*, and *An American Werewolf in London*, while selecting projects like *The Insider*, *The Sopranos*, and *RKO 281* - an HBO movie about the making of *Citizen Kane* - for feature stories which I wrote and edited for industry newsletters. Due to a combination of luck and timing, among all of the work, I have rarely accepted an assignment about which I did not feel passion.

Above all of this name-dropping, one thing must be stressed: I brought myself into the world of Hollywood entertainment media with virtually no connections, limited resources, and very limited finances. After years of banging my head against closed doors, I ventured to build my own house. To erect this structure, I knew that I needed to develop everything in my budding career from scratch. What I didn't know was that, three years later, I would be on Hollywood Boulevard producing a major media event. Starting in 1995, while teaching community college part time, I invented the means and the methods to becoming a self-made freelance writer, taking untested roads as I progressed. As such, I liken my endeavors to the concept of *sui generis* - that which arises and becomes something viable from nothing whatsoever beforehand. Create the myth on your own. Find in these pages an initiative to discover for yourself what may be possible as a freelance entertainment writer. Find a method of forging your own version of the journey. As a result of what should be a fulfilling, challenging personal experience, I'll look forward to seeing your writing in print.

Scott Essman
January, 2000

PARAMOUNT PICTURES STUDIO LOT

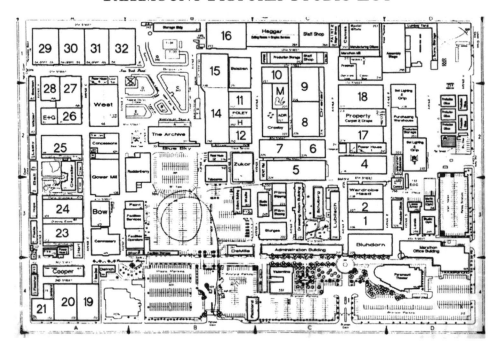

Chapter One

WHO IS THE FREELANCE WRITER?

First off, who is a writer? And what constitutes authorship? Are these important questions? Well, they are perhaps the most integral questions that a writer must answer before trying to blaze his or her trail in the craft. Knowing who you are and what you are trying to accomplish as a writer may be the key to maintaining the requisite focus, energy, and re-invention that one needs to sustain a freelance journalism career. My simple guidance concerning this matter is that the writer, using his chosen form of communication, actually has something to say about his or her chosen subject. In conjunction with that definition, the individual manner in which a writer expresses him or herself in a written piece is that which defines authorship. Call it a voice, an idiosyncrasy, or a style; as soon as one enters that stage of evolution, one has assumed the identity of the writer.

That said, the freelance writer is an unusual breed. Sure, writers come in all shapes and sizes. There are authors of fiction, newspaper beat reporters, contracted script doctors, entertainment magazine editors, 'roundtable' TV writers, spec screenplay writers, etc. Certainly, those are wonderful jobs - if you can get them - and writers within those circles have their own manners and modes. But the free-lancer is an altogether different animal. The word itself is an odd concoction of ideas, with "free" being its central theme. Yes, the free-lance writer is not tied down to any one writing situation, and thus theoretically "free" to pursue his own opportunities. However, getting writing assignments is often more a matter of not only finding them, but also inventing the work as he goes. While "standard" elements of writing exist in the freelance world, words such as 'pitch,' 'angle,' 'interview,' 'transcription' and 'deadline' regularly take on alternative meanings from those associated with regular writing gigs. Those terms, and many others, will be explained throughout this book as

1

they pertain to freelance writing. Of utmost significance, though, is to realize that you will be traveling on fresh terrain in the pursuit of a freelance career. The world of the freelancer is equal parts exciting, challenging, unpredictable, frightening, and propelling. In essence, freelance writers neither work for anyone, nor have anyone else working for them. They work for themselves. With that responsibility, you are truly free to make your own choices, but it is the type of freedom that must be closely guarded and carefully respected. And for each writer, let his or her own path be taken.

So why write on a freelance basis? For some, I suppose, the idea of hobnobbing with celebrities on *Entertainment Tonight* is potent. For others, the notion of riding down Sunset Boulevard in an exotic foreign car with 'you know who' on your cell phone is intriguing. However, there are more logical ways to achieve that level of 'success' than to enter the writing arena. The answer to "why write" is easy for me, as well it should be for anyone who wishes to be a freelance writer: writing is one of the most potent forms of self-expression. Discover something, anything, that you would like to say - that you must say - about a particular subject. In my case, the broad idea that I believed and wanted to express was that the craftspeople working in entertainment - the directors, writers, producers, special effects artists, recording engineers, editors, and many many others - were more vital to the creative process than had previously been acknowledged. This process has fascinated me since childhood, and I have consistently wanted to know how movies, recordings, TV shows, live events, and other forms of entertainment were created. As I endeavored to make my way as a writer, this was the natural territory for me to explore. What I did not know was how I was going to proceed, but I had at least defined my driving engine, one which still fosters my reason to be in this career. It follows, then, that I implore anyone contemplating writing as a career to unearth that which intrinsically drives him or her. Cement that notion as the focal point in all of your writing endeavors. And do so <u>before</u> you engage yourself to write about your selected subject.

2

Granted, there are writers and producers out there (some of whom I have unpleasantly encountered) who don't have any central personal issue as their motivating drive. Some of those folks have achieved fulfilling and successful careers, making more than a good living in many cases. Is their way the right one for you? On the set of a recent A-list film, a documentary producer actually told me, "anything for a buck." You decide. If it's the fortune and glory you're after, go for it. You won't be the first or the last, but those people come and go quite often in the world of high-gloss entertainment. If you are in it for the long haul, to foster a productive and memorable career, to create work that will be well regarded by your collaborators and colleagues, first discover your reason for writing. It will be the difference between a passing phase in your life and a rewarding career.

There are a few other precursors to setting one's writing goals. To reach long-term levels of success, one must ultimately have respect for the craft. It is unlikely that you would be reading these passages without already possessing this, but realize its relevance: you will be spending a good deal of time both in establishing a freelance career, and then in maintaining it, all while laboring at various writing projects, often under deadlines. Your financial rewards will often be less than stirring, sometimes nonexistent, depending on the assignment and the way in which you manage your career. But the risk-reward factor is one that you must carefully consider: if you value the written word and can appreciate when it is used well, your chance of reward dramatically improves. Of course, the converse can also be true: don't expect quick and easy rewards, especially if you haven't paid your dues. In equal measures, respect your craft and the people about whom you are writing.

Integral to your resulting development as a writer are three personal attributes, which will follow from respect: passion, patience, and persistence. Passion is often an overused, or worse, misused, term, and it consistently applies to the work of freelance writers. Invariably, the quality — and likely quantity — of your assignments

3

will directly reflect the passion that you infuse into your subject matter. In the body of my written work, those assignments for which I had the most passion stand out as my best stuff. I don't need to explain what occurs when one lacks passion - suffice it to say that the word "hack" is most easily linked to those who write about material for which they have no passion. Patience is an often-overlooked quality in a type-A world, but is a necessity in those parts occupied by the freelance writer. True, nice guys can finish last, but one would be amazed how corn does grow after the proper seeds have been planted (this concept will be further illustrated in coming chapters). In concert with patience — though, some would say, in contrast to it — is persistence. If one is persistent and exhibits that trait in a professional and respectful manner, previously unseen writing opportunities will surface. You will learn how following up on leads, networking among different contacts, and never letting a connection die are all part of building a fulfilling writing career.

So, what do you write? Only you can answer this. What subjects interest you? Music? Sports? Movies? What aspects of those fields do you find fascinating? If you feel those subjects have been over-covered or that they are impenetrable, then explore others, or perhaps focus on specific untapped parts of those areas. Don't be afraid to opt for choices that are less than obvious – they could prove to be a huge resource of information and personalities. As you will read plenty about, I had an interest and targeted goal of writing about special makeup effects artists who work in Hollywood. Much to my amazement, this was nearly virgin territory when I first started to explore my freelance opportunities in the mid-1990s, and the fact that so few people were writing about this subject was a key in getting my career started. There are a million stories in Hollywood past and present - search out those that have seldom or never been told. If you can find just one, you will avoid the harshest competition, find new audiences and avenues, and take your career in unexpected directions. Are you interested in technical material or more artistic veins? Both are interesting and both can serve your need for material. Are you predisposed to doing interviews with active or retired subjects, or do you wish to rely on historical records? Search your heart and find what moves you. It is a necessary first step in the pre-writing process.

Well then, let's say that you have found a focus and you have a writing direction. Now, how do you go about learning how to write? My initial training came from a small liberal arts college in the early 1980s prior to my tenure in and around the USC film school. Until that point, I had been a C student in English classes, with little real affinity for or ability in any practical form of writing. At my first college, the faculty had the interesting notion that freshman English should be taught on an interdisciplinary basis. That meant that a physics professor, Dr. Alan Russell, became my first semester freshman composition instructor. At first, I thought this was a maddening proposition as my class would be unduly difficult. However, Dr. Russell instilled in me a sense of the mechanics and structure involved in any written work. His tutelage proved instrumental in my gaining a facility for the writing process. I am far from a great writer, but I have reached the point where I have confidence in my ability. Over time, I have improved somewhat, but I know my limitations and strengths, and I have learned to play off of them.

Short of getting formal training in a college or adult education forum, I believe one can self-educate in this era. It is a given that to write well, one should read well. True enough, but I would extend that to say that the content of your reading material should relate to those writing areas you will pursue. For example, before researching and engaging in a specific subject, read everything in existence that you can about that subject. Was this material written well? Strengths, weaknesses, and areas which you can improve upon should become apparent. You will readily find books, magazine and newspaper articles, and some Internet material that constitute entertainment subject matter. Broadening your reading base is also beneficial; though my focus is entertainment writing, I read virtually every non-fiction source that I can get my hands on, regardless of its content. My shelf is lacking in

5

fiction, but I feel that the time I spend reading non-fiction material constitutes my leisure, research, and personal evaluation reading time rolled into one. Staying on top of how writers construct their non-fiction books and articles feeds both my passion and my profession. Read everything and anything that feeds yours.

In learning the fundamentals of writing, my soundest advice is to be pro-active, not re-active. Continually evaluate your current ability and need for further improvement. While it is true that one can always continue to learn, in the early stages of constructing your career, analyze the writing level of publications or outlets to which you might wish to contribute at some point. Does your writing ability seem up to these standards? If not, do you understand what you must alter in your writing - whether mechanics or style - to reach that level? Mechanics and technical aspects of writing can be learned — there are many books on the subject. Style is something that can be developed but must arise from somewhere. Usually, one gains a style after absorbing many different styles around him. This can take time, depending on how much you absorb and your capacity for intake. Be a sponge! Take it all in and your style will emerge. Give it time, nurture it, and you will likely witness the personal formulation of a style that is equal parts you, an amalgam of others' styles, and a bit that has come to you from some unknown (subconscious?) place. As you will see in Chapter 2, once you have a chosen subject and have started to explore your writing ability, there are a variety of venues for which you can write that will help you to more easily evaluate your position.

Chapter Two

BEGINNING THE PROCESS

Assuming that you have listened to that inner voice and gained, if not a specific direction, then at least a drive to start a career in entertainment journalism, you are ready to explore the possibilities and select some particular subject matter in the field. As such, ask yourself this: just what are the "Hollywood" media? In a broad sense, they are any enterprise — any "project" which involves the creative input of an individual or group — in the major media which function on a national (or, as is often the case, international) level, not necessarily restricting such operations to the physical limitations of Los Angeles. Currently, relevant media projects take place in New York, Chicago, San Francisco, Austin, Orlando, North Carolina and other cities and states, and the globalization of Hollywood has transformed the entertainment industry. In the 1990s, Vancouver, Toronto, London and Sydney all became prolific centers of Hollywood business, and this trend will likely continue into the 21st century. However, regardless of their ultimate destination and point of release/distribution, most media projects still have their origins in the Los Angeles area. As a result, for the purposes of this book, all such material will be referred to as "Hollywood" media, though the truth may be that those projects never actually come close to southern California. Taking that reality into account, the primary subdivisions within the Hollywood media are the following:

Motion Picture Production
Television and Video Production
Music Recording
Live Musical Performances and Videos
Live Theatrical Performances and Production
Radio Broadcasting
Print & Publication Enterprises

Sporting Events and Productions
Special Live Events
Promotional / Awards Shows
Amusements and Specialty Attractions

Keep in mind an important distinction: one can work as a writer *within* the aforementioned media as a viable contributor — you can be a screenwriter, television sit-com writer, radio copy writer and so on — and many of the career-building principles in this book may apply to gaining a foothold in obtaining such occupations. However, my primary objective is to advise potential writers in how to use these listed media as <u>target categories</u> for freelance articles, and maybe books. Hence, while one can certainly write as a writer *for* radio programs, musical productions, and television shows, this book concerns methods and practices of writing *about* them.

Certainly, any media within the Hollywood domain have the inherent advantage of sustaining a virtually immutable high profile. Writing about a feature film! This is almost as attractive (or should be to free-lance writers) as working *on* a film. Okay, maybe directing a film is infinitely more exciting than waiting on a set for an interview. But, in the Hollywood media at least, nearly every assignment in which you might engage guarantees that your writing will platform on a considerably large stage. People will see your work. It <u>will</u> get out there.

Yet in attempting to participate in such high profile venues as movies, rock and roll, or sporting events, where potentially millions are watching, there are several accompanying patches of quicksand. For instance, the larger the canvas, the more likely that others will be along for the ride in some form. Try getting onto a Spielberg movie, for instance. You can do it; I was on set for one. But when you arrive, there are already a billion other things going on — <u>Variety</u>, <u>The Hollywood Reporter</u>, <u>Rolling Stone</u>, *Entertainment Tonight*, and the network news are there. And that's just in one day. Okay, I exaggerate, but when you go for a swim in the big pond, be prepared to take a number and feel less than crucial to the lives of those you wish to interview and observe. In the fall of 1997, after a great deal of persistence, I was able to get a project that I had produced into the <u>Reporter</u> – my 30th anniversary celebration of the production of *The Planet of the Apes*. It was lots of work, but the editors there bit and it was very rewarding. The material was historically-based, and with the 30th anniversary tie-in, the staff saw it as relevant.

TECH*talk*

Creatures creators:
Renowned creature artist **John Chambers** recently enjoyed a surprise 75th birthday bash that turned into a who's who reunion among makeup-effects artists of the past several decades. Party host **Scott Essman,** who's writing a book titled "Creature People" about artists in the field, said: "It's also the 30th anniversary this year of the production of 'Planet of the Apes,' for which Chambers won an Academy Award for his creative makeup designs. That film broke ground for the way in which prosthetic makeups were produced and perceived by the industry."

After many phone calls, Scott Essman was able to get the <u>Hollywood Reporter</u> to include this item about his tribute to John Chambers and *The Planet of the Apes*.

9

In my experience, choosing less popular sub-sections within Hollywood offers you a chance to claim the selected piece of the pie as your own. You may even surprise yourself - when I got started, I never could have guessed that I'd be one of a very few writers striving to interview and write about makeup artists. As I ventured into other areas — writing about effects artists, directors and screenwriters — I was selective with my choices. Take stock of not just what it "hot" today, but what might be hot tomorrow. You could find yourself as the ONLY person covering your subject. I was amazed at how few people cared about historical material. When I did my *Wizard of Oz* tribute, for instance, I was the only guy in town who seemed to take notice of this film's 60th anniversary. Thus, for maximum exposure and access to your subjects, you should constantly be evaluating both your personal career position and the status of the various media before charging forward. Unearth current projects and "buzz" properties, then act accordingly.

If you don't already have a chosen subject in mind, before you can go much further, you must become a media sponge. They say that the business of Hollywood is small, and in many ways, this is true. It is not uncommon to meet people who, through a working relationship more often than a mere coincidence, know others who you might have met in your interviewing or production experience. In fact, it happens all the time. But in the International Alliance of Theatrical Stage Employees (the umbrella union that governs most actors, directors, writers, and craftspeople who work in film, television, and theater for Hollywood productions), there are over 35,000 active members in Los Angeles county alone. Add another 20-25,000 from the New York local unions, plus thousands more throughout the United States, and that constitutes a substantial number of potential interview subjects. Of course, there are thousands of additional non-IATSE members working in and around the different fields of entertainment, not to mention the thousands more who work in print, sports, radio and music recording who belong to different unions. Thus, there is no shortage of interesting figures who regularly engage in Hollywood-related activities, plus many more who operate on a local level but likely have interesting stories to tell. It's your job to conduct the research needed to locate them, find out what they do, and make contact. Often, you'll be shocked to realize how seldom these people have been interviewed. When I chose to explore the creation of *Willy Wonka and the Chocolate Factory*, I was taken aback when its editor, David Saxon, revealed that he had never been interviewed before. This is a man with 45 years of editing experience and not one article written about him! It's as if many notable Hollywood craftspeople are doing their thing, waiting for an eager writer like yourself to look them up and unlock their secrets.

Among the author's most personally satisfying projects was writing about David Saxon, the editor of *Willy Wonka and the Chocolate Factory*. Amazingly, Saxon claimed that no writer had previously sought to interview him.

What is the best method of finding these buried treasures? Personally, I have always been the kind of guy who — when I am not in the office with a stereo, computer, TV-video system, books, and magazines all working in a sort of simultaneous media cacophony — haunts libraries, electronics stores, book stores, music shops and newsstands in search of that which I don't already know about my subject (in fairness, I did this even prior to *having* a subject!). It has been said that knowledge is power, but that goes double for writers. And I'm not talking about a brief skim of the daily newspaper to gain information, reading that rare special article that cuts below the surface. Instead, I recommend total immersion. Read everything that's out there. You'll start to see the same books over and over as your travels take you to similarly stocked bookstores, but some titles will crop up for the first time after a while. This always happens with the first level of research - the most popular books, magazine articles, and Internet sites begin to resurface. Don't fret, because as you delve deeper, you'll start to get warm. Take lots of your own notes in the aisles or reading area of bookstores and libraries as you unearth new sources of information on your subject (do so discreetly or risk the wrath of the clerks). Then, start going further. Find those imported magazines. Go to specialized libraries, such as those at universities, and read trade journals and periodicals that exist about most popular entertainment/media subjects. Link to everything you find on the web to get to those secondary sources. Also, engage in the enlightening process of cross-referencing your sources and locate out-of-print books and industry-only resource directories and guides. You'll be surprised – I certainly was, when in 1995, I discovered a "special effects and stunts guide" printed by a small publisher in Los Angeles. This book, which took a while to dig up and even longer to order through an interlibrary loan (of which, I am happy to say, I am a local champion), was key to my first contact with the special effects and makeup community, and facilitated a year's worth of interviews and my first published article. Had I not dug as deeply, I would not have found this and other rare items that were integral to my early career. Chances are, if you are relentless in your search for resources, you will find that untapped gem that points you in the right direction.

As you start to hone in on your subject of choice, your writing inclinations and preferences will become self-evident. Are you most strongly drawn towards current projects? For many in the Hollywood pipeline, the greatest amount of attention and energy is funneled into the most recent films, TV shows, albums, concerts, and novels. A decided advantage to writing about a current project is that you increase your chances of gaining immediate attention from both publications and the people you endeavor to contact. Case in point, I was once stuck for a story idea after I had worked hard to develop a relationship with MovieMaker magazine. In their previous several issues, I had interested the editor in original article ideas and had them published. However, for various reasons I had reached an impasse regarding their yearly screenwriting issue. Several ideas — even some good ones — were discarded due to lack of interest on the part of the publisher or my potential subjects. Distressingly, I was faced with either devising a good article concept very quickly or allowing two months to pass by without participating as a freelance contributor – something I did not wish to do as it was still early in my relationship with the magazine. As I will often do to clear my mind and relieve stress, I went on a lengthy run into the California desert that Sunday morning. When I returned 45 minutes later I had the idea for my article — "Screenwriting in Digital" — a story about the manner in which the nascent digital effects technology has impacted screenwriters. Several writer colleagues approved of the idea, my publisher loved it, and I had a "green light" to get started. Then, two problems immediately arose: I had no idea how I was going to start the article, and I had 10 days to complete it. Luckily, I touched a nerve among the screenwriters who I researched and contacted, and four days later, I had lined up interviews with seven of the nine screenwriters I approached (in chapter three, I will discuss how I did so). One week later I had wrapped the article, plus I was the point man in wrangling all of the photos which accompanied my story (a whole separate assignment in itself). The angle in my article pitch was already hot on everyone's tongues and led to both a successful article and three ensuing article profiles that I wrote for MovieMaker regarding the "state of the art" of specific

13

craftspeople working in motion pictures – special effects artists, production designers and film animators. What started that particular string of articles was my initial screenwriting story – in that instance, writing about a provocative contemporary subject was freelance gold.

After placing a story idea about screenwriters in the age of digital effects with <u>MovieMaker Magazine</u>, the author was able to create several succeeding articles about Hollywood crafts with them. One covered the state of the art of film animation, profiling Brad Bird, director of *The Iron Giant*, pictured.

Then there is the concept of selecting a story idea from the "vaults" of Hollywood. Should you choose not to cater to the whims of the public consciousness, you are saving yourself a good deal of grief and stress. Your level and amount of competition drops off dramatically! News that seems outdated in Hollywood (and this can be in a matter of weeks - sometimes even days!) is usually left alone by the most media outlets. The scope of coverage in trade papers like <u>Variety</u> and <u>The Hollywood Reporter</u> rarely ever include historical or retrospective material, unless it involves an obituary (writers of these "appreciations" are often given the freedom to cut loose and offer detailed historical accounts of a person's work). Of course, if you choose to write about people or projects from the past, this may mean that less attention is given to your "outdated" material by magazines, newspapers, and other outlets to whom you pitch your article ideas. But historical Hollywood stories make for fascinating subject matter should they be treated with due care and attention to detail. Who could ever tire of stories about classic rock and roll? Golden Age filmmakers? Beloved stage and screen musicals? Great sports moments? Landmark events in radio/TV broadcasting? Any proper treatment of historical content will continuously be stimulating to audiences, and there is ample room for passionate coverage of relevant people and projects from the Hollywood vaults. As I have illustrated from the outset, my personal favorite projects are peppered throughout my career, and in several instances, proved to be my most memorable articles and events.

Another reason to avoid picking "hot" properties as your subject is that you are often at the mercy of the Hollywood publicity machine. In chapter seven, I will discuss the nature of publicists and publicity in depth. For now, suffice it to say that the lifeblood of publicity is wholly based on the clients' most timely needs, which often change on a daily basis! As this can foreseeably play havoc with a writer's agenda and deadlines, it is a sound idea to allow ample breathing room when working on a writing assignment which involves the latest movie, show, or album by a preferred artist. Have your niche pre-selected before diving into a hot property. Are you covering the art of the project or the artist himself? Will you be writing about the making of the property or the personalities who worked to create it? Principally, whenever an entertainment project comes into being, there are three elementary levels of production from which you should choose your subject:

1) The Talent (also called "above the line" in movies, or "performers" in music, theater, and live events)

Covering personalities will be discussed in chapter four, but at this juncture, it is best to state that I learned early that the more an individual's work speaks for itself, the more suitable that person will be as a subject. My first formal interview was with a makeup artist husband-wife team, Tom and Bari Burman, who didn't have a specific current project for me to cover so much as a substantial body of past work. Despite the lack of a "hot" property to discuss, the interview was an unqualified success - we covered landmark makeup movies such as *The Man Who Fell to Earth, Cat People*, and *Scrooged*. Therefore, you would be well off to choose a personality who is working within a selected project as your subject matter.

Tom and Bari Burman were the subjects of the author's first formal interview. In 1976, Tom created the makeup for David Bowie in *The Man Who Fell to Earth*, pictured. Since then, the Burmans have been among Hollywood's top makeup artists.

The U.S. is unquestionably a celebrity-oriented culture. These are the actors, singers, dancers, leading musicians, and some "star" directors, producers (in both film and music, and sometimes in television), and rarely, but sometimes, the writers! You can also throw in the top sports stars, who, in the frenzy of contemporary media junkets, are as crucial to Hollywood as most actors and musicians. The myth that all talent are celebrities is easily broken by a simple game that you can play yourself. How many movie stars can you name? TV stars? Musical acts? Out of that list, how many can make or break a project, either in getting it off the ground or in guaranteeing big numbers at the box office, in the Nielsen ratings, or on the Billboard charts? Pretty small number, isn't it? Interactions with celebrities are typically few and far between for writers who don't have direct access to them by means of, say, a standing gig with a major publication. Even so, for many celebrities, the fickle nature of Hollywood can render their tenure as top dogs relatively brief. Once you realize that there are merely a few hundred working actors in Hollywood — and quite a few less producers, directors and writers — who are "A" list (the most in demand of all talent), it dawns on you that covering celebrities is going to be, a) futile, as the media is oversaturated with such stories to begin with and b) unreasonably difficult, since you have a very small pool of people from which to choose as subjects. I have dealt with some celebrities, often inadvertently, and have found them fairly untouchable as far as getting formal interview time. In terms of gaining the access I would need to develop a proper written piece, it was an uphill battle. Most celebrity actors, athletes, and media personalities have a "team" of handlers, each of whom will question your presence in their "house." For a beginning writer anything is possible, but I would strongly advise looking elsewhere when choosing an initial course of action in plotting a freelance career. There are certainly many working actors and other talent who have *not* gained celebrity status — or who have sadly seen it pass them by — and you will pleasantly find that these folks are, by and large, accessible. Seek them out and you shall find them.

NOTE: If you are asked to pay money for a celebrity's interview time, simply hang up the phone and press onward. No interviewer, journalist, or writer should ever have to give a subject financial compensation for their time: remember, you need subject matter, but *they* are getting invaluable exposure when a written work is published about them.

2) The Craftspeople (also referred to as "below the line," or broadly defined, the technically skilled artists who physically put a project together)

These production workers include editors, recording engineers, stagehands, costumers, special effects coordinators, animators, cinematographers, digital compositors, set designers, orchestral composers and dozens more, plus those active directors, actors, and writers who are not widely afforded celebrity status.

As there are perhaps thousands of these talented folks roaming the alleys of Hollywood, this is the most logical category for subject matter. I will discuss the personnel in this group extensively throughout this book, as their work has been my ongoing inspiration and their stories my most compelling articles. Over and above that, after covering their projects, many of these artists have become my personal friends.

3) The Executives (sometimes unfairly called "the money" or "the suits")

Sometimes worthy of scorn but often integral to the realization of many Hollywood projects, executives include development people, supervisors, distribution experts, and other production managers.

Though I sometimes feel as though I am alone in this respect, I am of the school that an article can be equally interesting regardless of which of the three noted types of subjects are covered by a writer. In the spring of 1999, I interviewed studio executive Ted Hartley at the re-established RKO Radio Pictures, and this talk became one of the more fascinating, articulate interviews I conducted at the time. As you go forth, keep in mind that simply because an interview subject might be from an unglamorous discipline, it does not necessarily mean that the individual will be dull and the material uninteresting to readers. Instead, a written work's success has to do with the quality of the subject matter, the writer's treatment of the material, and the degree to which the written work is unique.

Ideally, if you have reached this stage of the process, you have decided on a potential subject, you have availed yourself of the variety of informational resources, and you have determined a course of action, be it current project, historical work, personality profile, or some other aspect of craft or craftsperson. Now it is time to assemble your research in preparation for that first contact.

Ted Hartley, current chairman of RKO
Radio Pictures, a studio executive who
became one of the author's most lucid
intelligent interview subjects.

Recently, I learned that before undertaking a screenplay, writer John
Logan (*Gladiator, Any Given Sunday, RKO 281*) takes all of his
resources, which he has cross-referenced every possible way, and makes
a massive timeline of every event that his subject matter encompasses.
This is a great idea for a writer in any medium, though it is time-
consuming. Ideally, when you set about to make your first contacts, as
I will describe in chapter three, you ought to have an internal knowledge
of your subject matter. Create a "bible", a master data base whether
written out as a flowchart, grid, or timeline, or perhaps as a list or
other format. You will refer to this tool quite often, and it will likely
ingratiate you with your subjects in ways that you cannot easily anticipate — they'll be impressed and comfortable with you if you can
demonstrate a true understanding of their work.

Fox Studio Lot

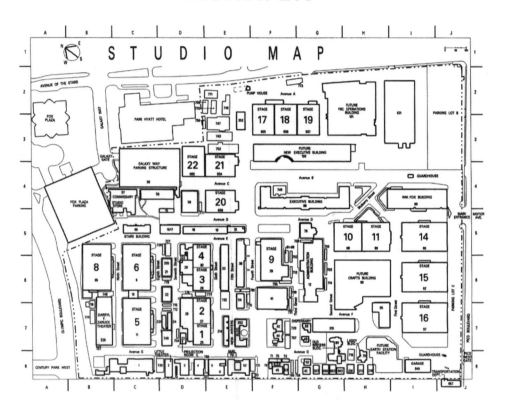

Chapter Three

MAKING THE CONTACTS
THE CONCEPT OF SUI GENERIS

sui generis (adj/n) of its own kind; constituting a class alone; that which comes into being from no previous precedent.

Though not mandatory, your career can be all of those things. There is nothing wrong with taking previously established paths to reach your goals, and they may work for you. But I have found that for every two successful authors, publishers, editors, and other freelancers in the writing world, there are two very different tales of "how I did it." Thus, and this is advice that will vary in its interpretation from writer to writer, don't be afraid to invent your own course. Define your position as a freelance writer. If you can see that your career is what you make it, your experience can be as idiosyncratic as you wish. Create a sui generis career for yourself.

In 1997, a friend from college who saw an ad for one of my projects contacted me. We shared stories of the ten-year gap since we had been in close touch, and she informed me of her struggles to become an independent filmmaker. "Even though I have had frustrations," she continued, "I call myself a filmmaker. Consistently, on some level, I make documentaries. I act like a filmmaker, and people treat me like one." This perspective can be easily adapted to your attempt to forge a freelance writing career, especially in a sui generis sense. Call yourself a writer, consider yourself a writer, behave like a writer, and others will treat you like one. If you act like some wanna-be screenwriter who's only doing this freelance entertainment journalism thing until the *real* Hollywood discovers you, chances are that people will not take your ideas or endeavors seriously. Even worse, they might not care whether you write or not. Make them care. Don't lump yourself in with others who exhibit no enthusiasm for their subject matter or their work. Be a *writer*.

Often, if you are passionate, focused, and committed to your subject matter, starting from scratch can be a good thing: nothing else can be compared to your projected path. Sometimes you will run aground with people who don't understand what you're trying to do. If you are dedicated, however, you'll find the people who get it, and they will appreciate you much more for trying something innovative. If you stick to the tried-and-true methods of becoming a writer - journalism major, internships, working as a gopher, copy editing, working up from the ground floor - best of luck and more power to you. But your competition will always be feverish, and you will have to work twice as hard as many of them to stand out from the pack. Mind you, I have nothing against hard work; in fact, I submit that creating your own sui generis writing track is more work than playing it safe and trying to ascend your way through the writing ranks. Yet I am too restless a soul to work within someone else's definition of progress. I didn't have a choice but to select the road less traveled.

My freelance writing experiences have been largely unique. While the mechanics of pitching a story idea, writing an article, and submitting it to a publication or other outlet might seem fairly standard, the manner in which I have come into many of my assignments can be considered sui generis. In most cases, I sought out story ideas and the proper avenues for their publication with no clear precedent in mind, either in my conception of the idea or in how I chose to present it. From out of the blue, for instance, in early 1996, I contacted <u>Cinefex</u> and pitched them on the idea of my doing a career retrospective of one of the many makeup artists who I had interviewed at that point. Through a personal reference I was able to initially contact the publisher, but realize this: prior to that call, I had never been published, nor had I written a spec article for any magazine. However, through discussions with the publisher, combined with my evident enthusiasm and the knowledge that I had accumulated in the months I had been doing my makeup interviews, that first phone conversation became my first published article : "Michael Westmore: BEHIND THE MASKS" [see Chapter 6 for analysis of that article]. What's more, the article led to three ensuing assignments for <u>Cinefex</u>. Of course, being placed in such a prestigious publication so early in my freelance career helped vault my reputation in the eyes of potential interview subjects and other industry magazines. Certainly, my relationships with some magazines, such as <u>MovieMaker</u>, <u>1stHold</u>, and <u>L'Ecran Fantastique</u>, began with their publisher/editors contacting me after they had seen something I had written which they felt was pertinent to the needs of their readership. But even in those instances, my methods of working with them was unorthodox; often, after discussing magazine content with the publisher, I would develop story ideas on the spot, leading to article assignments or pitch acceptances. After <u>MovieMaker</u> had discovered my knowledge of the history of movie makeup, they offered me the assignment of writing an overview article for them on the subject. But immediately after it was in the can, I pitched a medium-sized article about editor/composer John Ottman (*The Usual Suspects*) for their upcoming post-production issue. The Ottman piece, which they eagerly accepted, was based on an interview that I already had in the can for the premier issue of <u>Directed By: The Cinema Quarterly</u>, but I knew that there was enough material for a <u>MovieMaker</u> article as well. When <u>1stHold</u>, a fashion, styling, and makeup-oriented magazine, initially contacted me, their purpose was to obtain some quotes about my recent tribute to *The Wizard of Oz* (described in detail in Chapter 8). Sensing a new audience who I could reach through their publication, I parlayed my relationship with the publisher into several original articles and bartered ads.

Of all my writing anecdotes, my favorite sui generis experience is one that came very recently in my writing career, during the process of actually writing this book. Music is a subject in which I am very interested but have never formally covered. Since the early 1980s, I've been a tireless fan of most all types of recorded music, steadily amassing a huge collection of vinyl, cassettes, and CDs of all musical genres and styles. But I had never written about the subject, and I had always wanted to do so.

In early January, 2000, I spotted an ad for a live concert in the heart of Hollywood featuring two of my favorite musical acts of the past 20 years: headliners Dream Theater and opening act the Dixie Dregs.

When the author saw this poster in a newspaper, he determined to take his freelance writing career into the arena of music.

In pursuing this assignment, I was following a personal passion: I have always regarded Dream Theater to be the top band in the progressive-metal scene of the 1990s, with the Dixie Dregs established as one of the greatest instrumental rock acts of all time; this was too good a chance to pass up. I decided then and there to add to my repertoire of writing assignments and become a freelance music writer. Why not? I had enough confidence in my abilities and knowledge of the musical scene that I felt that covering this event could only enhance my professional resume. What followed were two weeks of calls, faxes, and confirming last minute details which led to the assignment. After contacting the venue to determine who was publicizing the event, I wound my way from the gig coordinators, to the promoter, to the record company, to the publicity department, to the publicist. Granted, publicists relish media attention, so they were quite interested in my desire to cover the event. Then I needed to secure a spot on *Nuvein Online*, a music-film-culture website with strong ties to Hollywood. I had written for them before (although only about film) and had a good relationship with the proprietor of the site, so after some reassurances, I got a "green light." I arrived at the gig, where tickets were waiting for me, and I had access to the bands and their resources through their respective publicists. Stirring my passions, I called myself a legitimate music journalist, acted like one, and got a dream assignment, all within a few weeks time. This is doable! It can happen. You can be the master of your writing destiny. Following is a reprint of my review of the concert, published in *Nuvein Online* #8 in early February 2000:

Keeping the Flames of Rock Alive
By Scott Essman

NUVEIN ONLINE Musical Review

Dixie Dregs and Dream Theater at the Palace Theater on February 4, 2000

Rock and Roll may indeed be dead, but superb rock musicianship was in full force last Friday at the Palace Theater in Hollywood. With the reunited legendary Dixie Dregs opening for progressive rock headliners, a group of skilled musicians showed a diehard audience that craftsmanship still counts in music. In the first of two shows, Friday's gig was packed with fans who had waited on Vine Street for hours before the powerfully entertaining show commenced, only to be sent home at 10PM sharp when the fire marshal suspiciously shut down the event (curious that a radio-sponsored dance had been scheduled for later that night). Nonetheless, with the teen fare and uninspired power pop that has been dominating the air and video-waves passing for rock of late, the *Dregs* and *Dream Theater* were decidedly a breath of fresh air.

Formed in the mid-1970s at the University of Miami, *The Dixie Dregs* were the ultimate eclectic instrumental band of their peak period. Led by guitarist Steve Morse, who often wrote every note of every song (for every instrument!), from 1977 until 1982, the band made records and toured relentlessly, spreading their brand of country-funk that was as much an ensemble effort as a show-case of the individual musicians' talents. Morse never relied on the hammer-on/pull-off pyrotechnics that every post-Eddie Van Halen guitar hero aped in the late 1970s and early 1980s; he strummed and picked his way to greatness with his amazing right hand and pulled off nearly impossible notes with his left. At the February 4 gig, which served as a reunion of many original band-mates, including bassist Andy West, who hadn't been with the group since the early 1980s, Morse, and the others, mostly in their mid-40s, still looked and played as if they were 25. Particularly riv-

26

eting highlights included a high-octane duet between Morse and fiddler Jerry Goodman (of the early 1970s *Mahavishnu Orchestra*), and an intra-group "battle of the instruments" that featured Rod Morgenstein's frenetic drumming and T Lavitz' graceful keyboarding. *The Dregs* (their name has been shortened on and off through the years) have just released an energetic CD entitled "Screaming in California," with live tracks recorded last summer at West LA's Roxy Theater.

Taking the stage after a limited break, *Dream Theater* gave its fans what they had largely come for: a concert rendition of their new concept album, "Scenes from a Memory." The 12 tracks, labeled as different "scenes" in each of two "acts," serve as a cohesive musical version of a play. It's as if *Dream Theater* has committed their own interpretation of a post-modern novel onto a CD. Told as a hypnotic "regression," the album is a sequel to "Metropolis," a track on their 1992 offering, "Images and Words." More polished and evolved on "Scenes from a Memory" than in their earlier recordings, *Dream Theater* pays musical and conceptual homage to bands like *Rush* and *Queensryche*, but, at all times, stands on its own. Throughout the Palace Theater show, *Dream Theater* engaged in fevered jamming, with John Petrucci's fiery guitar playing complementing the anchoring rhythm section of John Myung (a type of "rhythm bassist") and drummer Mike Portnoy (who co-produced the album with Petrucci). Portnoy, always in fine form, re-defines the concept of double-bass kick drumming for anyone who has witnessed a *Dream Theater* concert. Worth mentioning is keyboardist Jordan Rudess, new to the band, who provided lyrical solos and underscored Petrucci's intricate work. Yet it is James LaBrie's soaring vocals which hold the band and their tracks together; how many singers can you name who forge a unique identity with a crushing explosion of guitar-bass-keyboards and drums underneath? When LaBrie leaves the stage, which often occurs during *DT's* extended jams, the band is still exciting, but LaBrie's presence adds a unique highlight to *Dream Theater's* overall musical constructs.

27

Using the Telephone

The phone is your friend - really. The trick is how to use it. Through the phone, you will make contacts, network, pitch ideas, follow up on your leads, and finalize crucial deals. It's very true that writers should primarily rely on their writing skills, and with the prevalence of e-mail, telephone skills might seem less crucial. But to make vital personal connections, in lieu of personally appearing in someone's office, the phone is still the best method (perhaps we are not far off from high-speed Internet access which will allow videoconferencing, but let's face it, wouldn't you rather do an interview with a leading Hollywood director while kicking back on your living room couch in your underwear?).

Granted, cold calling people for interviews is often an iffy (and terrifying) proposition. You have to sell both yourself and the idea in one shot, and you often don't have much time to capture your subject's attention. If you have done your research, prepared your proposal, and are an effective communicator (which you ought to be on some level, verbally, considering you are a writer), you will often be heard out. That is, if you reach the appropriate person when you call.

Assuming that you have done the requisite fact-finding to know who to contact for your subject matter, and if you are dealing within the Hollywood borders, be prepared to patiently wind your way through the oft-unpleasant mélange of receptionists, secretaries, and personal assistants who often surround talent in all fields. And, if you're lucky and they will entertain your proposal, treat these people AS WELL AS YOU WOULD TREAT THE ACTUAL SUBJECT! This isn't only in the name of kindness and human decency (which, too often, people forget while buried in their personal agendas); this is also a career-saving method of behavior. Many such people have become my close friends and confidants and have facilitated relationships even outside of their own offices. Director John Landis' office, in fact, introduced me to such noted film historians and collectors as Bob Burns and Forrest Ackerman, leading to private trips to both of their wondrous homes!

Patience and persistence are operative words that will be mentioned again in this text - trust in both concepts, maintain the proper balance between the two, and your goals will be furthered. If you are clear as to what you want - a personal interview, a visit to a production site, or access to photographic material - you will likely succeed after a time. Here's a tip to remember - if an intake person at an office puts you off, assure them that you don't wish to be a bother, and be sure to ask when you should contact them again. Often, being dismissed (during a cold call, at least) is more a matter of bad timing than disinterest in your idea. If this subject is vital to your proposal, be sure to determine a better time to reach him or her. Be persistent - call them back stating your intentions, and you will find people responding to you. Often, you can chip away at that initially solid brick wall.

Writing Faxes

Should you contact the office of your intended subject and be forwarded to another location — likely a publicist, agent, or manager — be prepared to put your proposal into writing. Agents and managers have even **less** time to deal with you than the craftspeople or talent you are trying to contact. I was once told that one director's team of three personal assistants do nothing but manage that director's affairs 24 hours per day, seven days per week, leaving that director time to generate ideas, scout locations, etc. His situation might be the norm. What this means is that you must put your idea into written form to then send to the agent/manager/publicist. And while traditionalists still write and stamp letters and stick them in the mailbox, Hollywood offices probably consider most such pieces of unsolicited paper to be junk mail. In other words, get access to a fax machine! Okay, I resisted this act of conformity for the first six months of my career. But those 4:55PM rushes to the library to use their fax for $1 per page got old very quickly. Your fax machine will be your second best friend next to the phone. When writing faxes, adhere to three specific criteria above all:

1) Make your intentions very clear. In one particular pitch that went to screenwriting agents all over Hollywood (with mere days to receive confirmation of their clients' interest), I wrote in big bold letters across the top of the page:

"DIGITAL SCREENWRITING ARTICLE - XXX WANTED FOR INTERVIEW"

The fax went on to state the specific focus of the article - how writers must contend with the advent of digital technologies when they undertake a project, the name of the publication (after my pitch had been accepted by <u>MovieMaker</u> magazine), and the exact nature of the proposed interview questions. Within 48 hours of sending that fax out, I had seven of nine professional screenwriters lined up for interviews. Many told me that the clarity of the fax intrigued them.

2) Keep your overall proposal concise. Except for rare exceptions - the extensive writing project that requires a great deal of explanation - limit your material to ONE PAGE. This may sound harsh, especially to writers (like yours truly) who pride themselves on being completists, but the sad truth is that these folks who will be handed your fax (in an office shared by dozens of agents, publicists, etc.) will lose interest after the first page and may not read it anyway! Brevity is mandatory in a faxed proposal involving Hollywood talent and projects.

3) As much as it's possible, make your fax attractive. I don't mean to imply that it should be dolled up with photos and fancy graphics, but you did pick up a book with "'Hollywood" in the title. Make use of your font sizes – key in large letters for the most important information, leave plenty of space for the lesser ideas, and make your contact information at the bottom of the page clear and easy to read. Don't **ever** make the potential subject work hard to understand what you are trying to do. Get them (and his/her agent) excited about the project. Your idea is vital to that person - tell him why. So many people are only intrigued by what's "hot" in the public eye. But, as in Chapter 2, I have

discussed why the field for writers covering the hottest properties may be already full. Instead, find an angle on your subject that isn't necessarily the latest project from the hottest artist. Indulge yourself in your conception of a story: what about this subject is new or different or vital to readers? My "digital screenwriting" story for <u>MovieMaker</u> wasn't directly related to any one current project, but it was a prominent concern of most screenwriters I contacted and facilitated discussions of each screenwriter's relevant new projects (for more information, see my article in <u>MovieMaker</u> #33, Volume 6 - April-May, 1999). In fact, for that article, the publisher informed me that I had written a "sexy" fax. It never crossed my mind that it was sexy, but that fax did initiate the entire process of creating the article.

The Snowball Effect

As you make contacts, strategically network through your subject matter and you will gradually experience a snowball effect - one contact can lead to several. You can make a contact that leads to another in the same field or perhaps in another field entirely. You may even find yourself travelling in circles you never knew existed. My initial contacts in the film industry were with makeup artists, but these contacts eventually led to similar connections with people in special effects, then screenwriting, editing, and directing. The message is to not limit yourself - when you finally get onto a project and have become acquainted with your subject, introduce yourself to the other personnel working on the project. Regardless of your subject matter, don't be afraid to explore its various dimensions. When I covered the visual effects for *Mighty Joe Young*, for example, I flew to the Bay Area to interview the personnel at two special effects studios, covering how the movie was made and what digital technical advances were pioneered to create a realistic giant gorilla. Those interviews, plus other technically oriented interviews conducted in the LA area, would have been adequate to complete my article. However, I then made sure to seek out the director, producer, and even the studio executive involved in the project. It was my biggest project to date - literally the 800-pound gorilla - but I thought that it was primary to learn all that I could about the many dimensions of the project. Though the effects were my written focus, I wanted to know everything that I could about the film. The article was a difficult assignment of 15,000 words, but I was complimented on the extensive nature of my interviews, both in the type of subjects I covered and in the depth of each interview. It is noteworthy that the article, which was a cover story for <u>Cinefex</u>, was the result of my branching out from my focus on film makeup, through concentrated connections and networking. Also, it led to a future liaison with RKO Radio Pictures, as they were the re-formed company that produced *MJY* in 1998.

Mighty Joe Young was the author's first cover story for <u>Cinefex</u> Magazine and the biggest assignment of his career, the result of strategic networking and research.

Forming a Constituency

Gradually, after accumulating a sound body of work, people will begin to take note of you. With this comes respect from your peers and colleagues, as well as potential interview subjects. Bob Schiffer, one of the longest running department heads of any studio, recently told me, "You're getting famous." I had to laugh, since I am well aware that I am a very little fish in a tremendously oversized pond — an ocean! — but the fact that he had seen my work in a variety of magazines was uplifting. Make sure that while making contacts and watching the snowball start to roll, you maintain your creative and technical balance, as much as possible - try to cover as many different Hollywood subjects as you can without overloading your plate. This can be tricky and more work than it sounds, but it can only help you to diversify and expand your potential markets. As much as I am grateful to the makeup community for becoming their resident groupie (or, as paramount makeup artist Rick Baker calls me, a "makeup geek"), I feel as though it has only helped me to cover other subject areas. Purposefully, I have managed to cover a healthy mixture of subjects - young and old, historic and contemporary, big projects and small ventures. Get past the obvious - never discount a retiree or a newcomer as a proper subject. You can never tell when an interview subject might become a very exciting eye-and-ear-opening interview. As a result of my choices, I have good contacts in all areas of Hollywood and have garnered what I feel is a wonderful group of colleagues in the industry. While I wouldn't call on many of them to bail me out of jail, I feel as though I can call on most of them for professional advice, support, or information. And, surely, I can contact nearly all of them to be future interview subjects.

33

Chapter Four

PREPARING THE INTERVIEW

Integrating Your Research

While it's true that you might be a better interviewer if you know nothing of a subject going into a meeting, I would not recommend this course for new writers. Sure, you can discard notes and reference material once you are physically in the interview. But to prepare yourself for the eventual task of transforming a transcribed interview into cohesive written material, it's helpful to understand the most important events, projects, and figures pertaining to your subject matter. If you're endeavoring to contact a cinematographer about his newest project, your entire connection with that person might rest on how much knowledge you have about his previous projects, relevant movements in the field, and crucial innovators in the recent and remote past of cinematography. Much is riding on your ability to speak intelligently of this material. If your legendary subject refers to his Academy Award-winning film and you didn't even know that he won an Oscar, how can you gain his trust? When you get to the interview, you should have the following at your fingertips:

1) A detailed question list, whether to be used as reference notes if the interview takes place in person, or as a direct group of specific questions from which you will read. The more time you spend on this list — no matter how self-assured you may be in your ability to improvise questions and follow-up answers with more in-depth questions — the more confidence your subject will have in you. Ultimately, you want to set him/her at ease, and knowing your content will achieve that.

2) A cross-referenced guide to the person's resume of projects, with a list of personnel, themes, or other consistencies noted. In other words, uncover the actors, studios, and craftspeople whom the subject you will be interviewing has selected as collaborators. When I met Paul

Verhoeven for a career retrospective interview, it was crucial that I discuss his use of two primary cinematographers, Jan De Bont and Jost Vacano, on nearly all of his Dutch and American films. The unveiling of this fact became one of the more interesting strands of discussion in the interview and led to a follow-up discussion of his visual craft and technique. I had noted that Verhoeven had a war theme in several projects: *Starship Troopers* evoked his Dutch epic, *Soldier of Orange*, with the former substituting giant space bugs for the latter's Nazi antagonists. Under the auspices of merely covering *Troopers*, as it had just been released when I met the fiery director, we conducted an engrossing two-hour session. As of this writing, I am planning to publish the entire interview plus a new segment in the Summer, 2000 issue of Directed By: The Cinema Quarterly.

PAUL VERHOEVEN INTERVIEW

Film	Year	Cinematographer
Dutch TV	1960s	
Business is Business	1971	JPB
Turkish Delight	1973	JDB
Keetje Tippel	1975	JDB
Katie's Passion		
Soldier of Orange	1978	Jost Vacano
Spetters	1980	Jost Vacano
The Fourth Man	1982	JDB
Flesh + Blood	1985	JDB
Robocop	1987	Jost Vacano
Total Recall	1990	Jost Vacano
Basic Instinct	1992	JDB
Showgirls	1995	JOST VACANO
Starship Troopers	1997	JV

* STARSHIP and SOLDIER OF ORANGE are similar in that there is a common faceless monolithic enemy who it seems cannot be beaten. The difference is the take on WWII patriotism, STARSHIP being sardonic about the willingness to fight but ORANGE being true. Is this due to the difference between working in America and Holland?

* What was the process of deciding which shots you would achieve practically with ADI/Yagher and which were to be CGI?

* What do you communicate to the effects people during shooting?

* What creative limitations do you have when you collaborate with an effects supervisor like Phil Tippett?

* How much technical knowledge of Tippett's effects are necessary to direct the sequences that featured bugs?

* How difficult was it to match Tippett's work to ADI's live action bugs on set?

* What is your working relationship with the human effects supervisors, such as Rob Bottin and Kevin Yagher?

* At the time of ROBOCOP, Bottin was a legendary designer - how much did you delegate to him in getting the look of Robocop? (same with Tippett and animation for ED-209)

* Bottin's effects in TOTAL RECALL may be his most remarkable -
was that from the script/whose designs? (head, Cuato, winged arm)

* Why was Bottin's stuff was cut from the original BASIC INSTINCT?

* Do you find the desire to return to recurring themes in your
work, such as the femme fatale characters in SPETTERS, FOURTH MAN,
BASIC INSTINCT and SHOWGIRLS?

* Is it a creative or personal decision to work with the same crew
and actors on successive films, such as Jan De Bont, Rutger Hauer,
Rob Houwer, Rene, Monique, Stone, Eszterhas and now M Ironside?

* Do you believe sex has as much dangerous qualities as alluring
qualities, as per TURKISH DELIGHT, SPETTERS, FOURTH MAN, TOTAL
RECALL, BASIC INSTINCT?

* Why does sex also has amusing qualities to you - 3 breasts TOTAL
RECALL, sexual jokes in STARSHIP, and shadow play in KEETJE TIP?

* Was the character of Nomi in SHOWGIRLS consciously drawn similar
to Katie in KEETJE TIPPEL? Also BASIC INSTINCT?

* Monique Van De Ven (TURKISH/KEETJE) and Renee Soutendijk
(SPETTERS/FOURTH) were both very capable and beautiful actresses;
why not use them in US films - you or others?

* Do you feel responsible for Rutger Hauer/Jeroen Krabbe breaking
into US films as notable actors if not huge stars?

* Any attempt to publicize Dutch films - hard to find! Releases?

* FOURTH MAN is more direct and uninhibited than BASIC - are you
catering to a new audience here or are you attracted to new ideas?

* What qualities did Jan De Bont exhibit in his films with you
that forecasted his work as a director?

* STARSHIP and SHOWGIRLS both have a crisp, shiny look as per Jost
Vacano. Do you choose a DP depending on his look or other tools?

* Dutch TV - All Things Must Pass <u>1979</u>
(WWII resistance leader Arie is shot by Dutch SS; 35 years later
revenge by Arie's comrades; former communist joins in execution)

* Body of work since ROBOCOP is sci-fi except BASIC/SHOWGIRLS,
which fit into Dutch films. Any conscious effort to take a project
now, or is it project by project basis?

* Houdini or Ulysses with Phil Tippett?

The author was armed with this information sheet when he met director Paul
Verhoeven for a November 1997 interview.

A promotional poster for Paul Verhoeven's 1997 film *Starship Troopers*, the project for which the author was able to gain an interview with the Dutch director.

3) Recent material about both you and your subject that you can integrate into the session, especially if it's in person. One producer once told me, "in this business, inundate people with whom you want to associate: while this does not mean dropping a pile of papers in their laps, if you can demonstrate that you've found a photo from one of your subject's early projects or early influences, they will realize that you've done your homework." With that type of trust established, your interview can go in unexpected exciting directions. Also, if you show some of your own written or production work that the subject might relate to - technically, aesthetically, or otherwise - that could foster new connections between the two of you and open up new avenues of communication.

Sticking to the Work at Hand

One key to establishing comfortable ground rules with potential subjects is to guarantee them that you are only interested in talking about the work. Whether you're interviewing an actor or a sound engineer, tell them straight out that you are restricting your questions to craft. Unless they touch upon work-related issues, avoid all personal matters. You wish to maintain a courteous professional manner. This isn't to say that you can't have fun and get loose in the course of an interview; I often interject humor and "mock" questions to break the ice at several points in a session. After Chris Walas described the torturous process of creating dozens of little rubber monsters for *Gremlins*, my follow-up question was, "Did you beg them to do the sequel?" Many such non-sequiturs can also ease the tension of difficult interview sections. But always be aware of lines that should not be crossed. Never ask a subject with whom they have been sleeping: don't ever become associated with checkout stand tabloid journalism. Also, if there is a preliminary meeting prior to an interview, share your methods with your subject - show him or her the equipment and interview tactics you will use. If subjects show an interest, familiarize them with your system — on several occasions, I have actually handed subjects my mini-cassette or Digital Audio Tape (DAT) recorder and sometimes give them the tape itself to examine. Let them hear how they sound in the headphones. They will appreciate it and feel more a part of the overall process.

Maintaining Communications

Chiefly, the way in which I gain my subjects' trust is to earn their respect. If they ask for a fax of the interview questions, send them one. If you have followup questions about the material in a written work that features their name, call them. You'll be glad to clarify any confusion, and they will be glad to set you straight, rather than finding an error in print later on. This sharing will create positive two-way exchanges that will result in them calling you with information. After I had gained enough trust with the makeup community, I would get calls from people who wanted to include me in *their* projects and events. If you fail to get such calls, do not take it personally - remember that these can be among the busiest people in the world. One costume technician working on *Mighty Joe Young* told me that while she's on a project, she has "no life," implying the nearly round-the-clock nature of working on a big-budget film; when she's off of a project, she could go "months on end without working." However, staying in touch with your subjects, especially if time has gone by from the time of the interview until its publication (or perhaps its non-publication if the project has been unexpectedly delayed) is important to the upkeep of your various professional relationships. After I had several dozen interviews with makeup artists in the can for my book/video project *CREATURE PEOPLE*, I saw months go by while trying to land a book deal. Though I was able to publish several articles about make-up artistry over the next year, I was concerned about losing touch with many of my significant subjects. As a result, I embarked on a series of special live events which I hoped would bring the makeup community together (more on that in Chapter 8), and I still regularly send my subjects customized holiday cards with updates on my various endeavors. It has worked wonders in the name of showing my numerous subjects that I am still alive, productive, and am striving to publish that book!

The Persistence Factor

In terms of getting through to potential interview subjects, there is a fine line that you must walk: persistence is everything, but being pushy will get you nowhere. While there is nothing wrong with continuously calling a place of business in a polite manner, asking if they have had time to consider your proposal, you never want to become a whiney pest. That is the best way to invite total exclusion. After a first fax of mine caught the eye of director John Landis — whose *An American Werewolf in London*, *Thriller*, and *Coming to America* were prominent films with regards to special makeup effects — he called me and expressed interest in granting an interview when I was further along.

Over the next several months, I contacted Landis' office, representing myself with more authority on my subject matter with each successive contact. By this time, I had built up a nice body of interviews. Most times, he was predictably busy, but after one rewarding morning in which I interviewed director Joe Dante (*The Howling, Gremlins, Explorers*), I called Landis from a pay phone on the Paramount Pictures lot. I waited anxiously as Landis shuffled his afternoon schedule to accommodate me. An hour later, I was in his office asking him about his blockbuster-laden career. He even opened the interview with a previously taboo makeup secret - he revealed the identity of the person behind the famous Bigfoot "documentary" film footage from 1967 (for the answer, see <u>Cinefex</u> #71, September 1997). When I thanked him for the interview and impromptu scheduling arrangement, Landis said, "You were persistent; never pushy, but persistent; that's good." So long as you don't become an annoyance, if you want to reach a subject badly enough, and your intentions are upstanding, in the words of Winston Churchill, "never, never, never, never give up!"

Dealing with Rejection

So you've been persistent, but the doors have been closed. Evaluate your situation. Have you represented yourself appropriately? Have you demonstrated knowledge or interest in your subjects? Have you given the subject(s) ample time to find time for an interview? Have you considered an introductory gesture prior to requesting an interview - have you faxed or mailed him/her information about you and your intentions? If you have done all of those things and are still rejected, you may be facing a true brick wall. In 1996-1997, I interviewed every makeup artist in sight except one: Rob Bottin, the makeup effects wizard behind *The Howling, Robocop,* and *The Thing.* It seemed that Bottin no longer entertains the mainstream press, and I was lumped in with them. After many attempts to reach him with no luck, I finally shelved the idea. It seems that "no" is his final answer. Then again, sometimes "no" can mean "later" in Hollywood, especially if your subject is under the gun of a deadline or particularly difficult project.

When I first sought interviews with makeup artists, I contacted many of the top shops and studios around town, seeking out the best in the business. The office staff for one of them brushed me off almost completely at the beginning, so badly, in fact, that I considered it a ·dead issue. The lead artist at that studio was makeup expert Greg Cannom, the genius behind the Academy Award-winning work in the films *Bram Stoker's Dracula* and *Mrs. Doubtfire*. However, being persistent, I called the studio again after a few months, and was at least able to get a "try us later" response. A few months later, I had gained the trust of another worker in that studio who encouraged the supervising staffer to at least hear me out. Soon I was on the phone with him preparing the interview, and a date was set. As I was preparing the interview the day of the session, I met Cannom in the hall. He was cautious and reserved and informed me that he had recently been burned by another magazine. I started to realize why this interview had been difficult to arrange. As we sat down to start the session, he informed me, "Well, I have about an hour to do this." Sensing his hesitancy, I made every effort to put him at ease and reassure him that I was both a fan of his and most curious to cover his entire career on tape. The hour passed and I stopped the session. "We can keep going," he imparted to me, and another 90 minutes later, we finished the interview, having covered everything I wanted. Unbelievably, we had hit it off so well, over the next two years, the subject and his initially-disinterested staff hired me to create three demo videotapes of their makeup highlights, and they have become one of my closest allies in the makeup community to date. Since then, I have written feature articles about Cannom's recent projects, including *From the Earth to the Moon*, *Bicentennial Man*, and *The Insider*. In this case, at least, a brick wall crumbled, and persistence most definitely paid off.

Chapter Five

CONDUCTING THE INTERVIEW

Making the Connection

If you have diligently conducted your research, made your initial contacts, and properly networked and expanded your milieu, you will at last arrive at your interview, hopefully prepared as described in Chapter 4. The next essential element in the freelance writing process is to conduct a fulfilling interview. As the quality of an interview is directly related to the degree to which you connect with your subject, there are several elements of the interview process which you should carefully consider. A personal interview is highly recommended; though a phone interview can be rewarding — perhaps the best option when dealing with a shy subject who might prefer the anonymity — your ability to reach your subject and uncover the heart of a potential story usually increases during a face-to-face meeting. That said, it is also recommended that you meet the subject in his/her place of work: you'd be amazed at how the willingness to reveal treasured craft secrets and the ability to recall them increases exponentially as you physically get closer to the place where the work originated. Suffice it to say that holding an interview session in one's private studio, office, or even at a production location is truly preferable to meeting someone for coffee at a crowded, noisy, nondescript restaurant. Subjects will often offer to meet you at public places; it is reasonable to politely request an alternative meeting at their creative epicenter. Call it karma or the action of the subconscious - subjects are stimulated in their work environments much more so than in other locations. Sometimes, you will be invited to their homes; I have interviewed numerous directors, editors, film composers and other craftspeople at their houses, and this usually works well. The general idea is to have very little external interference so that you facilitate as comfortable a conversation as possible. Of course, trying to arrange an uninterrupted interview in a subject's place of business might prove problematic. This is often the trade off, and I have learned to be patient and turn off the tape recorder if a subject gets an urgent call or visitor. Usually, the best run offices will make sure that you are not disturbed during an interview. I've even had subjects tell important callers that they were in a "meeting" with me and that they'd call back later. In one case, a director told the executive producer of a TV show that he was too busy with me to talk for very long!

Unearthing the Passion

My rule of thumb in any writing project is that I am always the most curious person on the planet about my subject matter. Regardless of the subject or assignment, I have a consistently tireless desire to know more about my subjects. Whether this is fabricated or not is unimportant (though it helps to have your own passions about the material); if you have a genuine interest in your subject as you conduct an interview, you will get beyond the obvious questions and begin to delve into some valuable terrain. As you do this, you will stir your subject's inner passions and bring out some of the "gold." Keep this in mind throughout your interviews - most subjects are in their respective career positions because **they truly care about their craft.** I have met the rare Hollywood artist who is in this position purely due to luck, ego, or nepotism. However, the vast majority have generated a career because their love of the craft matched their talent. Knowing this, you, the interviewer, are responsible for uncovering this inner passion. If you do so, even the humblest of subjects will start to talk about his work. After all, they have granted the interview for a reason, and you must find that reason and adequately exploit the chance to uncover it. Hollywood people are usually more forthcoming as they get more in touch with their passions. Given that, you will naturally become more involved in the interview as they do.

IMPORTANT NOTE: Because you possess the ability to lead your subjects into potentially vulnerable spots - i.e., uncovering their hearts as you drift into discussions of their early beginnings, for example - it is crucial that you maintain a level of professionalism as you do so. Chances are they have only just met you prior to the interview, but in a few minutes, they may be baring their souls to you! Do not take advantage of this position in any manner lest you jeopardize your entire career. Word of mouth works two ways, and the last thing you need is a reputation as someone who is profane, vulgar or distasteful during personal discussions – don't corrupt the faith that the subjects have shown when they let you into their world. Also, if you have stirred up your subject's passions as described, it is best to avoid subjects of a financial nature — how much they get paid on a project, what their working budgets are, etc. — unless that is crucial to your eventual written piece. Last, but not least, until you have gotten to know your subjects well, do not presume that they are going to help you beyond giving you this interview. I once had an assistant who, during an inspired section of an interview about artistically succeeding under budgetary pressures, asked a subject if he would consider working on a planned low-budget film! I almost lost it! This is the last thing that a subject wants from you — they want you to tell their story, not hire them for your personal needs. One last point: don't EVER ask them to get you a job, especially when you barely know them. Nurture all your relationships with interview subjects.

Going with the Flow

There are as many types of interview subjects as there are people in the world. Very few will be similar and no two will be exactly the same. You must be prepared to analyze your subject within the first few minutes of the session and properly adjust to his or her demeanor in a Q and A situation. The "one-word" answer will often occur and can rattle you at first - you ask a detailed, thoughtful question and all your subject can say is "yes" or "no." Now what do you do? I've been confronted with the problem on occasion - at one point, very early in my career, I had conducted a preliminary interview in which I saw the person's portfolio of creative work. But during the full interview session some weeks later, he closed up on me, perhaps due to self-consciousness about his word choices once the tape was rolling. If you have done your homework, as I had in that instance, you should be pre-pared to ask a series of follow-up questions to the one-word responses. If nothing comes to mind, a simple "Why?" usually provokes further explanation. Conversely, I have done some interviews where I hardly had to ask *anything*. I would start out with a "so then, your next project really took your career in a new direction..." and before I even had the chance to implement my inquisitive tone, the subject started to give me a ten-minute answer. You cannot possibly imagine the difference between an interview transcript consisting of a series of one-word answers with desperate follow-up questions to an interview with pages upon pages of information from a question you didn't even ask. The most forthcoming subjects are always your best since you will have much to choose from when you get to the writing stage. However, don't be afraid to control such interviews. If you are after specific types of information, politely stop your subject and describe your particular needs. Do not, however, attempt to force your subject on the material at hand - this is your problem, not his or hers. Listen to what they are saying. This may sound like pointless advice, but your management of an interview is intertwined with your level of concentration on and comprehension of your subject's responses. Given that, so long as you receive a suitable amount of answers that follow your intended interview path, give your subject "breathing room" in the interview - allow him/her to discuss things which may not seem relevant on the surface. First, you never know when backstory or tangential informa-tion will be useful to you later, and secondly, often a conversation can lead to surprising gems when it drifts off of topic. On several occasions, I had been asking technical questions of my subjects that led to other all-encompassing strands of discussion. Let's say you ask a sound effects editor how a particular piece of digital sound equipment works: that may unveil an amusing story about something that went wrong during the process of recording sounds for his newest movie or TV show. Allow those stories to come forward, and backtrack if you failed to understand something said earlier in the anecdote.

The Art of Invention

Many times during an interview, you will refer to your notes, or read from a question list. However, after a few interviews are in the can, you will begin to get a sense of the dynamics of an interview: how much time you will need, the type of information you will get from the subject, what directions the interview can take. You will capitalize on these types of intuition and become a better interviewer over time. After a while, you may get such an innate feel for a subject, you will be able to discard notes entirely and base the entire session on the research and preparation that preceded the interview. You will invent questions that are of equal importance to your subject and the writing assignment itself. Sometimes, an interview that relies on improvisation can lead to a completely unforeseen writing project. Case in point: in the Fall of 1999, I took interest in a book of photographs about the innovative film *Baraka*. Through the book's publicist, I contacted the author and set up an interview with him about the assembly of the book. In my research, I discovered that the author, Mark Magidson, not only produced and co-edited *Baraka*, he also produced the landmark IMAX film *Chronos*, which is one of my all-time favorite non-narrative films. During the interview, in which I covered the process of producing the book, we entered into a lengthy discussion of the mechanics of the IMAX film format, the creation of both *Chronos* and *Baraka*, and the world of large-format non-narrative cinema. Both a fascinating interview track and a rich source of information, the session was enough to stir my interest in an entire "state-of-the-art" article about large-format films, which was subsequently published by MovieMaker magazine for their April-May 2000 issue. From that one book that caught my eye, a simple interview tangent metamorphosed into a seven-month, five-interview process, including sessions with a production company and several technical support personnel, and the facilitation of a large publicity firm. The lesson might be to let your imagination take hold of you during an interview - within reason, of course - and allow new courses of potential substance to develop.

From a simple interview about the creation of a book of photographs from the ground-breaking non-narrative film *Baraka*, the author developed an entire article on the large-format filmmaking process.

Creating Your Transcription

Right off the bat, the first rule of thumb is quite simple: transcribe your entire interview word-for-word, if possible. Transcription can often be a drag - it is typically a time-consuming process. If you can type 60-70 words-per-minute, there is usually a 2:1 or 3:1 ratio of transcription time to interview time on tape. Ideally, if you have lots of time on your hands (which you will NOT have if you are an active freelance writer), it is best if you transcribe an interview yourself. For one, you will undoubtedly hear things that you don't remember hearing during the interview. One's concentration may be sharp during an interview, but gaps in memory will still occur; forgetting something is part of being human. Also, as you listen and write, you will possibly pinpoint the best stuff from the interview, saving you time in the editing process. Listening to an interview a second time, plus writing it as you listen, will dramatically improve your understanding of the interview's key points. If you don't have the luxury of time, you will need to send out your tapes to be transcribed. Expect to pay between $15-$25 per hour for transcription time, depending on the assignment. In my career, I have had five different transcribers, some good, some bad. Bad means that they take forever to finish a tape, give you incompatible file formats, and overcharge you! In other words, as with everything else in modern America, you will have to search hard and go through some trial and error before finding efficient help. In the best possible world, you send off your tapes and receive a complete transcription via e-mail that you can immediately start reading and editing. If neither you nor your transcriber has time to completely transcribe an interview, you will be forced to "search and destroy" through your tape, meaning that you will have to listen to it and only transcribe quotes which will be useful to your written piece. If this is the case, the advice is again simple: the more carefully your interview is transcribed, the easier your life will be in the editing stage. You will have to glean quotes and information bit by bit, and assemble them into some cohesive whole. This is never the best choice, but you will be put into this position at some point if you write long enough on a freelance basis (or, I surmise, on any basis!). Then, after all is transcribed, you must start to edit.

Editing Transcripts for Time & Content

When I was writing my 15,000-word *Mighty Joe Young* article in the summer of 1997, I was faced with plowing through interviews with six people from one effects studio, four others from another studio, four artists from a matte painting firm, creature designer Rick Baker and his key mechanical designer/puppeteer, the chief gorilla suit performer, the film's director and the producer. Did you count 19 separate interviews? That's a great deal for one article, and it was an overwhelming task to attempt to work with so much material. After stumbling on several first tries, the only way I could possible engage myself in the project was to bury myself in each separate interview transcript and begin to find the most relevant information, whether in directly quotable form or as background facts for my set-up and expository sentences. Even if you don't have as large an assignment as I did on *MJY*, I suggest that you edit all of your transcripts for crucial content before you write one original word. You will likely find that several sections of the final article will be buried within an edited transcript. Eventually, these sections will be the building blocks of your final written piece. Elimination of unwanted material should be instinctive - is your subject stating an opinion or fact that clarifies the subject? Enhances it? Sheds new light on someone else's point? Is she or he making a technical point? Is it stated clearly enough that it can be a direct quote? If not, can you understand the statement well enough to write an original sentence which incorporates the item? You will get a feel for this procedure as you embark on freelance assignments. As your career develops, you will gain the facility for cleverly shaping your interviews so that you get the best possible information from your subjects. You will ask questions that you know will lead to a good introductory quote, a good closing quote, and quotes about specific elements of your project. Obtaining the skill of differentiating between clearly useful/potentially useful/practically useless information in a transcription is also beneficial and will improve with time and effort.

When you are really rushed, you may have to madly scan through an interview, picking out the one or two quotes that you can add to your nearly finished article before it must go out to meet your deadline. Worse, if you have so little time that you can't even put the subject onto tape - a last resort - you will have to directly write down/type into your computer what is being said to you in person or over the phone. This hasty process is never recommended, but you can get into these situations and have little recourse. I once typed a subject's exact words INTO THE BODY OF AN ARTICLE as I was making final proofreads and edits. It wasn't the best idea, but I worked his words in, and it helped the article and allowed the subject to express his point about the material.

Sometimes, you will complete a transcript and realize that the information is either a) too thin to justifiably incorporate it into an already rich uniform article, or b) too good in and of itself to merely bury it in a big article. Your intentions might have been proper in contacting this subject and involving him/her in the process of your story idea. However, there is a solution to having an insufficient amount of material (or overabundance of good stuff) in a transcription: the sidebar article. On several occasions, I have sensed that an edited item would be better used as a full sidebar to an article than as an incorporated part of a larger whole. Of course, you need to clear sidebars to approved articles with your publication, but most times, they are glad to have them. A sidebar is usually an attractive item to format, and can often break up a page in an already lengthy piece. Earlier in this chapter, I recalled an article I had written about the IMAX film process. In the throes of creating that piece, I interviewed musician Michael Stearns, who had scored several large-format films that were referenced in my article. However, even during the interview, I sensed that the details on Stearns would get lost in the midst of a technically-oriented article about shooting, editing, and manipulating oversized film stocks. Hence, I proposed a sidebar on Stearns, based on my interview. Granted, he could have had a whole article devoted to his career, but the time and situation were right for the sidebar that follows:

In the course of transcribing your interviews, you may determine that some subjects are better served as their own sidebar items, such as this one that the author wrote about film composer Michael Stearns for an article about large format films.

51

<u>Sidebar for MEGA-MOVIES: The State of the Art of Large Format Films</u>

MEGA-MUSIC - Michael Stearns creates sonic atmospheres for large format films

"You can't help but suck up the environments that you are in - they become part of you after a while," said composer Michael Stearns of his world beat vibe. Stearns is a unique musical performer and producer in that he specializes in scoring and creating soundscapes for large format films in his Santa Fe, New Mexico studio. "I have developed a huge library of sound over the years. That gives me an edge in doing these types of projects."

Starting his musical career as a guitar player, Stearns first found his true calling with the introduction of synthesizers in the early 1960s. "I was self-taught, mainly since there were no schools," he said. "When I heard the first synth recording, I just wanted to jump on and go. The sounds that synthesizers created truly shaped my experience."

Among Stearns many large format triumphs were writing, performing and mixing the music for *Chronos*, a three-month process, and writing original music for *Baraka*. "*Chronos* was unusual in that the music was written before the film was edited," Stearns explained. "On *Baraka*, there was a lot of writing music to picture. I was on the project for a year and nine months. Both of those projects are one of a kind — the music has a life of its own."

In collaboration with co-composer Christopher Hoag, Stearns has actively worked on numerous large format films, including "ride films" such as *Back to the Future* and *Star Trek: The Experience*, for which he often serves as soundtrack supervisor, creating the sound effects as well as the music. What sets Stearns apart, though, is likely his integration of sounds and music from all over the world. "In my travels, I got to see that music in other cultures is closely related to ceremony and spirituality, not linked to pop culture," he said. "Rather than focus on Western music, I have synthesized ideas from many different cultures and made something new out of them."

Sometimes you will conduct an interview with the specific purpose of creating a sidebar or, perhaps, an informative "box" that accompanies your article. In this case, a transcript must be whittled down to its most essential core. In the case of the IMAX piece, a publicist coincidentally contacted me at the time I was finishing the piece. Among her new clients was James Stern, the director of a new IMAX film: *Michael Jordan to the Max*. What great timing for them, but it was way too late in the game (no pun intended) to incorporate the project into my article, and I already had my sidebar completed. Instead, my publisher gave me a few extra days to create a "box" for the Jordan film and other notable upcoming IMAX releases. Compared to writing and editing an article, or even a sidebar, interviewing a director for a box item is a cakewalk. Given the late entry of the item, I could have easily dismissed the whole concept of the box, but I knew that a Michael Jordan IMAX project was relevant to my IMAX feature and could only further inspire the magazine's presentation of my material. The result was a well-rounded section of article, sidebar and box:

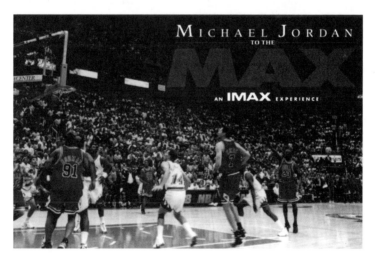

After the author had wrapped his article and sidebar about IMAX movies, a publicist approached him to write about the director of a Michael Jordan IMAX-themed movie. The piece became a "box" addendum to the completed mother article.

SPOTLIGHT: COMING SOON in the IMAX format –

Michael Jordan to the Max

From versatile producer-director James D. Stern (the upcoming feature *It's the Rage*), this 45-minute film chronicles Jordan's final championship playoff run in the spring of 1998. Over a three-month period, Stern — who, being a huge basketball fan, became a part-owner of Jordan's Chicago Bulls in 1985 — shot with three cameras at every game, amassing 500,000 feet of film. A combination of sports performance, behind-the-scenes footage, and over 30 interviews, the movie will open May 5. "Jordan's story is extremely dramatic," said Stern. "We use the playoff run to cut back and forth to various stories from his life." Next for Stern is producing an IMAX film version of his popular theatrical show, *STOMP*, due in 2001. "We want to take that show and expand it for IMAX," he said. "We are going to collect sounds and shoot in places all over the world, and those sounds will come together in a *STOMP* performance at the very end of the film," Stern revealed. "That's something that you cannot do on stage, and I think it will be enormously educational and cool."

A note about transcribed computer files: though you may wish to save ALL ORIGINAL TRANSCRIPTS in their raw form, as you proceed through the transcript editing process on the journey towards the writing process, create new files for edited transcribed work. For example, though my first file was:

<baker mjy transcript.doc>

 - my edited version of that transcription, with all unnecessary quotes and information eliminated, might read:

<baker mjy edit.doc>

Having new transcripts separated from original ones will create less confusion in the often-chaotic stage of assembling a final article. Also, by no means should you think that you're finished with the original document. You will regularly be required to return to the original transcript for clarification, to obtain quotes that you might have at first eliminated, or to comprehend what your subject said (after you incorporated it into your edit, you may have lost sight of the quote's initial intention). With edited transcripts in hand, you are ready to embark on the intense, laborious, uplifting process of creating a final written work.

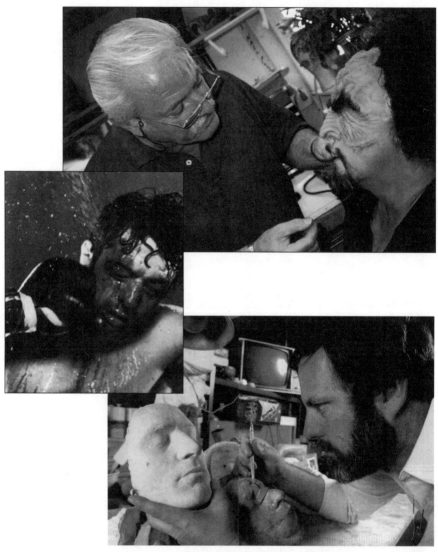

For the author's first published article, his chosen subject was Michael Westmore, whose makeup career has spanned 40 years and numerous awards. Pictured are Westmore preparing Robert DeNiro's extensive makeup for *Raging Bull* and Dave Quashnick making JG Hertzler into the Klingon warrior Martok for the TV show *Star Trek: Deep Space Nine*. Westmore has been the makeup supervisor for all *Star Trek* TV shows and films since 1987.

Chapter Six

WRITING THE FEATURE ARTICLE
(STORY/REPORT/ESSAY)

You have reached the writing summit. At this point, you have isolated your intended subject matter, adequately researched the topic, and thoroughly interviewed the key person/people involved, if and when possible. Your article (often called a story, report, or essay, but essentially the same concept) is lying around you in various disorganized pieces and sections, waiting for you to assemble it into a cohesive, logically compiled whole. You have done all of the legwork and must face the actual writing process. Now what? Be mindful of some essentials both before and during this stage.

Your purpose is to inform, entertain, and intrigue

One should never forget the audience. When you first endeavor to create your article, be aware that - though you write alone for hours upon hours, seemingly doing so for nobody but yourself - others, especially given the high-profile nature of the material, will be reading it some weeks or months later. Therefore, you ought to carry with you the responsibilities that accompany your task. You are sharing this subject with others, much like a town crier. Hence, you are informing them, first and foremost. Yet don't forget the essence of the material: to entertain. For those who have higher aspirations with their writing, there is the idea of intriguing your audience as well. Not every article fits into the proposition of audience intrigue, but the potential to give your readers ideas beyond those on the printed page certainly exists. Without becoming too pretentious, it is feasible for one to set such a lofty goal for an article. It is certainly one of the purposes of any type of writing, freelance entertainment articles included.

Surpass the superficial - invent

You must have a fresh take on your subject, and you must get past the obvious right off the bat. There is no gentle way to communicate this thought: to spend the time and energy on a work that just skims the surface of the material is a complete waste of effort. You must dive into the material and offer your audience an idea that they did not - could not - know about the subject before reading your piece. For example, the IMAX Corporation does not exclusively produce IMAX films - they are merely one of several companies that do so, with the most prolific being MacGillivray Freeman Films in Laguna Beach, California. I learned this and did a profile article about MFF and the entire IMAX process for <u>MovieMaker</u> magazine that served to enlighten my audience.

Among the author's articles for <u>MovieMaker</u> was a profile of MacGillivray Freeman films, one of the primary producers of IMAX format films such as *Dolphins*, pictured.

Speaking of which, when you offer information of a rare sort, anticipate your audience and offer them new (hopefully new) information. Did my readers know that the re-make of *Mighty Joe Young* had an in-joke for true buffs - that the theme song from the original film, "Beautiful

58

Dreamer," was being played by a saxophonist on the beach in the new film? I didn't think they did, so I told them. Real fans will love you for peppering your work with tidbits of little known facts and revelations, and your inclusion of these elements will only enhance your material. Also, the best writing will manifest itself when you create a personal take on your subject. Of course, you will develop or discover a style in your writing, which will understandably permeate and identify your various articles, but a consistency in your writing style should be continuously evolving. Too many uninteresting entertainment articles are the products of rote thinking, as if the writer felt as though the subject matter and not the writing itself would be enough to satisfy readers.

Know your competitors

Why write at all if not to go beyond that which is already in print about your chosen subject? In the early stages of my writing career, I had been assigned to write an article about a big-budget studio movie and was starting to set up interviews with the principal crew people. Not long after the assignment had been made, I received an FYI package from the publisher containing many other articles about the film. At first, I was unsure exactly why I had been sent this material, so I called the publisher to find out what he wanted me to do with the stuff. He said that his modus operandi - whenever writing an article himself and for his magazine in general - is to read that which has been written about the subject in question, then set out to write the definitive story about the same subject. I will modify his thoughts and suggest the following:

1. Read everything that you can get your hands on about the subject. If it is a current project or contemporary personality you are covering, there should be useful materials in bookstores and newsstands. If your subject/subject matter is historically based, you may need to access libraries and Internet resources, always a greater challenge. You will quickly find the range from well-written, useful materials to sloppy, nearly useless junk. But never discard anything about your subject since you never know until you sit down to write what might come in

59

handy. That essential minor detail that fills in a blank just might come from the most seemingly useless book. Keep it around until you've sent off that final draft. This means that you must become something of a pack rat - keeping magazines and newspapers (or at least the significant articles in them) will save your life some day if the subject matter in them becomes one of your writing assignments.

2. Catalog all research materials. The few hours that you spend making sense of the information you have collected on the subject could make all the difference when incorporating those elements into your article. One useful method is to create a master outline and methodically work off of it. As discussed briefly in Chapter 2, as you go through your magazines, books, Internet bookmarks, etc., you should note where each item fits into your different outline sections. If each separate item is coded with a number/letter system that corresponds to similar numbers and letters on your master outline, assembling a large article could be a more clear and simplified process, which is particularly vital if you're on a difficult deadline.

3. Discard everything in your research except the factual information. Besides wanting to avoid plagiarism more for aesthetic reasons than legal ones - you also have your own unique perspective offering a wholly original look at your chosen subject. This makes detachment from all of the other books and articles not only logical but also necessary. Facts are facts, and once you have checked and cross-referenced them among all of your sources, use them liberally in attempting to tell the true story of your subject. True, research is a vital tool, but *you* must ultimately be the source of the written idea as it appears on your pages.

Determining the length of the article

Having read other articles about your subject and with your goal for the article firmly in mind, you must decide on its length. There are three ways which this usually transpires, and all are crucial to your assessment of the amount of time it will take to complete your article:

1. Let the market dictate the article length

This often occurs if you are writing completely on spec or if you have been given few guidelines from your intended publication. You have a story in mind, but how much is there to write on the subject for the target audience? I have written for such a variety of outlets, my determination of an unassigned article's length is wholly based on my knowledge of the audience. You can't write a 15,000-word article, no matter how engrossing the subject, if the magazine you have targeted regularly publishes shorter feature pieces. Chances are, if your story is to be the primary one - the cover story - you'll know in advance and be told the desired word count. Also, if you have received an interview assignment from the publication and are to transform it into a feature article, you may be asked to "see how much you can squeeze out of it" to determine your word count. Once you have had some practice, it is a safe bet that for every hour of interview time, you can create 1000 words of written material.

2. Consult with the editor/publisher in advance of writing

Most often, you will be given a firm word count if you have been assigned an article, and you are usually held to that amount. Seasoned editors know what they are looking for and often start making editorial and layout decisions prior to your final article submission. If you pitch a story and it is accepted, in all likelihood a specific word count will be dictated to you.

3. Begin estimating based on interview/subject matter

As your freelance career develops, you will start honing your ability to judge the eventual length of your articles considering the resources from which you will be working. I can usually tell how long one of my articles will be based on the nature of my material and how in-depth any interviews or research materials at my disposal have been. My basic rule of thumb is that a solid 90-minute interview of good information can be transformed into a thorough 2000-word article, which is a basic medium-sized piece. If an interview hasn't gone as well (the subject is not forthcoming, the material is thin, etc.), you are likely going to need additional interviews with other subjects. However, often a transcription will defy your expectations - you must see it on the page before you can assess your needs for supplementing a key interview with others.

Offer overview of subject/subject matter

However specific your article will get - and ideally, most will get very specific, replete with direct quotes, first-hand accounts, and researched facts - you should assume that your audience has a minimum amount of information about your subject. In general, setting up your story with a background and establishing context for it builds the reader's confidence in your ability. The amount of overview material you include is often dictated by the size of the article, the exception being overview articles themselves, for which the reverse is true (relatively little specific information supporting the general overview material). Typically, a meaty 5-7 sentence introductory paragraph will suffice to establish your subject and initiate your leading idea.

Choosing a lead

A great mystery in the world of the entertainment/media article is creating the compelling lead. Yet the colorful nature of most personalities and projects gives you a leg up on the average news article. The idea is to make your lead inherent to the material. A few tips:

1. Offer a point-of-view

This doesn't necessarily mean your point-of-view; it just means some point of view. There is a good chance that, in discussing the person or project that constitutes your subject, someone you have already interviewed has offered an account of the subject which was interesting, succinct, and appropriate to your unique treatment of the material. Find it!

My lead for an article about Rick Baker's Oscar-nominated work in the Eddie Murphy vehicle *Life* in the spring 1999 issue of <u>Make-Up Artist Magazine</u>:

"Few films in the history of cinema feature singular collaborations of performer and makeup artist."

It was simple and to the point, but it facilitated a discussion of Jack Pierce and Boris Karloff (who together created the original Frankenstein monster and the original Mummy for Universal Studios), and led into a discussion of Baker and Murphy, who collaborated on *Coming to America* and *The Nutty Professor*, leading to three Oscar nominations and a victory for Baker's work.

Another example, from a feature article about animation in <u>MovieMaker</u>:

"Consider how many timeless cinematic moments are conjured from pure animated fantasy."

This lead was followed by several examples - *Lady and the Tramp*, *One Froggy Evening*, and *How the Grinch Stole Christmas* - which set up my story of contemporary animated work.

A third example of one of my actual leads:

" 'IT'S ALIVE!' are inarguably among the most unforgettable words in American cinema, and the impact that they made on horror films with their appearance in *Frankenstein* (1931) is incalculable."

This intro, from an article for <u>Creative Screenwriting</u>, established a foundation from which I deconstructed the script and screen versions of the movie, comparing them and offering a historical perspective on the material. While my leads are not earth shattering, they simply set forth my article ideas and give the reader a context for my approaches to my subjects.

One of the author's leads to an article concerned the original screenplay to *Frankenstein*.

2. Locate an appropriate quote

Success in #1 above should ultimately deliver you to a quotable item that could set up your whole story, if not in the very first sentence of your article, then somewhere in the first paragraph. Sometimes the entire article can be set in motion by the early inclusion of a good quote, and often readers are hooked in by such a lead.

"Eddie Murphy has the unique ability to bring my work to life," was a direct Rick Baker quote (with double entendre since it inadvertently referred to the film *Life*) that I knew was going to be gold in my final article. For more information about finding quotes, please see Chapter 5.

3. Bookend article with closing quote

Much like the opening item in an article, an ending quote gives your story the proper parameters of a well-written piece. If your interview has gone well, the subject, without excessive prompting, will often offer a summarizing statement that should ideally:

a. reiterate the lead
b. end the article on a high note
c. leave them wanting more!

One example that comes to mind is my original closing quote by Rick Baker for my <u>Cinefex</u> article about *Mighty Joe Young*. Though the publisher added an additional closing paragraph for political reasons, my closing served several purposes and maintained the uncluttered tone of quotations that I had achieved throughout the article:

"...one reason I wanted to do this show... was to build a better gorilla suit than we had ever done before. Joe is definitely the character that I've always wanted to create."

Fitting quotes into your article - not vice-versa

One of my publishers liked to tell writers that articles should be in the neighborhood of 50% quotes - let your subjects tell their story; writers should make sense of the story, its chronology, and keep it flowing, but they should not imprint their own version of the events on the material. While this philosophy is not applicable in every instance, it informs the writer about the importance of direct quotes - they will ultimately become the lifeblood of most articles.

A well-conducted interview will contain many usable quotes, but in every case, they must be carefully selected and assembled into your article. Often, you must edit quotes due to space limitations and because most people do not talk in an interview format as cleanly as you would wish for inclusion in an article. Spend a healthy chunk of time cleaning up your transcripts and they will serve you well.

In the best of all worlds, after your interviews and research have been completed, you have had enough time and distance to digest the material, thoroughly read through your transcripts, and think about different angles your story can take. If this is so, it is of primary importance to you to make sure that you write your article, and not let the article write you. Too often, and I am guilty of this on more than one occasion, time and pressure constraints find writers conducting interviews, transcribing parts of them, and desperately searching for quotes to structure their story all within days (hours?) of a deadline. The result of this type of experience is a finished product that, while it still has the chance to be engaging, is somewhat compromised. One should avoid the last-minute shenanigans that accompany hasty compilations of "greatest hits quotes," where any original writing appears merely in service of stringing together a series of interesting quotes. While that may sound interesting, writers must force themselves to properly structure their particular version of the story, and then fit quotes from their interviews into their article as needed. The careful eye can easily distinguish this type of article from the former.

Proofreading 101

Professional writing means proofing all of your work. In the day of the spell and grammar checker, there is little reason why your manuscript should have more than minor errors when submitted for publication. In addition to going over it oneself, the writer should invariably pass his or her work along to a fellow writer or trusted confidant for proofreading purposes. Even a competent lay person will do - anyone with a reasonable reading level is capable of detecting mistakes in the basic use of grammar, syntax, etc. And you should surely be aware of the spellings in your own subject matter, or you don't actually know your subject well enough to be writing an article about it! If you don't know your stuff, you better have LOTS of resources handy or you're bound to dig yourself into a deep hole. You will begin to smell of the worst form of small-town newspaper hackwork! That said, writers are at the mercy of their publishers and editors in terms of how the received documents translate onto the printed page. Again, your experience with different publishers will likely run the gamut from meticulous to sloppy, so you must get accustomed to the dynamics of the publishing process.

MICHAEL WESTMORE

BEHIND THE MASKS

article by Scott Essman

Star Trek is more than Paramount Pictures' most successful franchise. It is also the dominant presence on the Paramount lot in the heart of Hollywood. Currently comprised of two weekly television shows and an eighth feature film just completed, the *Star Trek* empire inhabits nearly one-fourth of the studio's expansive soundstage and office space. In one of those busy, cluttered offices, *Star Trek*'s supervising makeup artist, Michael Westmore, relaxes behind a desk reserved for fielding phone calls and watching video dailies.

The Westmore name has been synonymous with film industry makeup since Michael's paternal grandfather, George, established the first motion picture makeup department in 1917 at Selig Studio, later to become MGM. In subsequent years, six Westmore sons made their mark in the industry: Mont, Michael's father, was Rudolph Valentino's makeup artist and supervised the makeup on *Gone With the Wind*; Frank worked for Cecil B. DeMille; Wally created Fredric March's makeup for *Dr. Jekyll and Mr. Hyde*; and Ern was a staple at RKO Pictures. But the two uncles who influenced young Michael the most were Perc — who created Charles Laughton's *Hunchback of Notre Dame* makeup — and Bud, who in 1945 succeeded the legendary Jack Pierce as head of Universal's makeup department.

"I hung out at Bud's house on the weekends while I was going to college," Westmore recalled, "and in 1961, he offered me an apprenticeship at Universal. The first thing I worked on was *Flower Drum Song*." Westmore soon became the first apprentice for makeup great John Chambers, working on features such as *The List of Adrian Messenger* — where character makeups disguised the familiar faces of Tony Curtis, Frank Sinatra, Kirk Douglas, Burt Lancaster and Robert Mitchum — and in television, making up actors for the classic monster comedy, *The Munsters*. When Chambers went to

Veteran makeup artist Michael Westmore has won an Academy Award and nine Emmys in his prolific thirty-five-year career.

Twentieth Century Fox in 1968 to create the primate makeups for *Planet of the Apes* — for which he won a special Oscar — Westmore remained behind and was promoted to head of the makeup laboratory.

After leaving Universal in 1970, Westmore spent the next five years researching therapeutic cosmetic aids for scarred accident victims and individuals with birth defects. From there he segued into his first stint as head makeup effects artist on a film — a little project nobody else wanted, entitled *Rocky*. Directed by John Avildsen, the movie was written by and starred an unknown Sylvester Stallone. A rags-to-riches tale set in the arena of professional boxing, *Rocky* would require makeups suggesting fighters' injuries. "I met Stallone over at MGM," Westmore recalled, "and he wanted to see some-

thing quickly. So I took a can of wax and created a swollen eye on him. He liked it, and that was the beginning. I made a cast of his face and started right away."

As the only makeup artist on the low-budget film, and with little time to prepare, Westmore enlisted Stallone's help in researching the fight sequences. "Sly got some old 8mm fight films and took them to his apartment on Sunset Boulevard. There was a punching bag hanging from the chandelier in the dining room, no furniture, and a big dog that ruled the house. In the bedroom, there was only a mattress on the floor. We sat on this mattress, with the door shut and the blinds drawn, watching these fight films and taking notes." With the films as reference, Westmore designed makeups for Stallone and Carl Weathers, who portrayed rival Apollo Creed. "When we were shooting the fights, I'd put Sly in one chair and Carl in the other. I'd make an eye piece for Carl, glue it on, color it, and then hand him the hair dryer so he could dry his eye while I was doing Stallone. I'd go back and forth between the two of them."

Despite its bargain-basement techniques, the film — and Westmore's makeup work — received undreamt of accolades. "Everybody was shocked

CINEFEX 68 ▶ 29

ANALYSIS OF ACTUAL ARTICLE

In December 1996, my very first published article appeared in <u>Cinefex</u> Magazine, a quarterly which features detailed accounts of special effects in major motion pictures, TV shows, commercials, and special industry projects. Not having written about this subject matter before but eager to become associated with a prestigious publication, I pitched my article (first page below) to the publisher, based on an excellent interview I had recently completed with famed makeup artist Michael Westmore. The process of rewriting covered over six months and five drafts from start to finish. In the next several pages, I will offer an overview of each actual draft, highlighting the corrections and describing the rationale behind them. It must be understood that the ultimate goal of this process is to arrive at the best possible version of the article, ideally with the final draft retaining the author's original conception for the article. After the implementation of minor changes, key deletions, and significant word-choice suggestions, the article is clearly improved from draft to draft. The minor alterations that occurred with each ensuing version of my story were created in the natural continuum that is the rewriting process.

"Michael Westmore's 35 Years of Masks"

Introduction

"Star Trek" is more than just Paramount Pictures' most successful franchise ever; it's also the ~~most~~ ~~domineering~~ ~~force~~ on the Paramount lot ...

Prior to writing the bulk of the text for this article, I endeavored to start the process with a handwritten draft of the introductory paragraph. Note how my original words contain structure but are essentially a brainstorm of sentences. The editor chose to make necessary corrections and suggestions to help establish my subject. After a

69

basic addition of an apostrophe on the first line, a major word change is suggested, from "most domineering force" to "dominant presence" in describing *Star Trek's* impact on Paramount Pictures. Next, the editor questions my use of the term "worlds" when describing *Star Trek*, asking me, "consisting of what?" Note that, a few lines later, I used the term "empire" which, while crossed out, will become the substitute for the word "world" in my next draft. Several suggested edits follow, with the editor using arrows to indicate continuations of my thoughts. He commutes my phrase about "the Hans Dreier building" to a later, more logical point in the article and recommends shortening a sentence describing the subject "fielding up to 100 short phone calls." Finally the editor comments on some descriptive phrases, asking me if I want the subject to "look" relaxed, making a straight deletion, and informing me that three included adjectives are "repetitive".

Author's Draft - July, 1996

Michael Westmore's 35 Years of Masks

by Scott Essman

<u>Star Trek</u> is more than Paramount Pictures' most successful franchise ever; it is also the dominant presence on the Paramount lot in the heart of Hollywood. The <u>Star Trek</u> empire inhabits nearly one fourth of Paramount's expansive sound stage and office space. In a quiet private office within the Hans Dreier building, Michael Westmore relaxes behind a modest desk reserved for fielding phone calls and watching video dailies. Westmore has been preparing for the eighth <u>Star Trek</u> feature film in addition to supervising the makeup and creature effects for both the <u>Voyager</u> and <u>Deep Space Nine</u> television series. On the eve of his first location trip to Arizona, he reflects upon his 35 years working as a makeup artist for film and television.

In the submitted draft of my first paragraph above, note the many changes that were made subsequent to my initial hand-written draft. Once the editor got hold of it, she took the liberty of re-writing the material and sending it back to me for my perusal. Several changes were made, in the overall name of refining and condensing (the inherent job of an editor). Note below that the changes all retained the spirit of my draft and improved the writing without tampering with my ideas.

First of all, it was cleaner to eliminate the word "ever" when describing the aforementioned most successful franchise of *Star Trek*. Second, the specific description and location of Michael Westmore's office was altered to allude to "one of those quiet, private offices" of its kind, giving the reader an idea of a type of office and deleting the name of the building, a trivial item in an opening paragraph. Next, Westmore's specific duties are summarized in an opening sentence phrase without including the particular names of the TV shows. Also, the concept of Westmore supervising makeup and creature effects is held off in that sentence. In the final change, by simply identifying him as a "supervising makeup artist," the redundancy in my final two sentences is excised and the paragraph is shortened. Also notice how the editor ends the paragraph with my exact words from an earlier sentence.

Editor's Draft - September, 1996

Michael Westmore: Behind the Masks
Scott Essman

Star Trek is more than Paramount Pictures' most successful franchise; it is also the dominant presence on the Paramount lot in the heart of Hollywood. Currently comprised of two weekly television shows and an eighth feature film in production, the *Star Trek* empire inhabits nearly one-fourth of Paramount's expansive sound stage and office space. In one of those quiet, private offices, *Star Trek*'s supervising makeup artist, Michael Westmore, relaxes behind a modest desk reserved for fielding phone calls and watching video dailies.

Recognize the changes from the editor's draft above to the final publisher's draft below. First, the publisher eliminated the semicolon in favor of ending the first sentence with a period in its place – a stylistic choice more than a grammatical correction. The second change is one based on the change in time from the article's inception to its publication; the eighth *Star Trek* feature film had been completed in the ensuing months. Next, the publisher corrected an error that both the editor and I overlooked: we each repeated the proper noun "Paramount" three times instead of reverting to the common noun "studio" which the publisher astutely put in its place. The last two changes are made with the publisher exercising his creative and professional license. He felt that it was appropriate to change the described concept from a "quiet, private office" and "modest" desk to that of a "busy, cluttered office" and simply "desk" for the supervising makeup artist who is in the article. Although it wasn't my observation that the office was "busy" and "cluttered" and it was my remark that his desk was "modest," the changes properly set the stage for an article about a person whose daily life is quite hectic. Is it playing with the truth? Perhaps, but it merely paints an accurate introductory portrait of the subject and his working life.

Publisher's Draft - December, 1996

MICHAEL WESTMORE
BEHIND THE MASKS
article by Scott Essman

Star Trek is more than Paramount Pictures' most successful franchise. It is also the dominant presence on the Paramount lot in the heart of Hollywood. Currently comprised of two weekly television shows and an eighth feature film just completed, the *Star Trek* empire inhabits nearly one-fourth of the studio's expansive soundstage and office space. In one of those busy, cluttered offices, *Star Trek*'s supervising makeup artist, Michael Westmore, relaxes behind a desk reserved for fielding phone calls and watching video dailies.

73

cinefex

12/6

Dear Scott —

Thanks for your input on this issue. I think it's a really nice article. Looking forward to the one on John Chambers.

No need for you to send a copy to Mike Westmore. I'm sending a few direct to him.

Best wishes,

Don

Don Shay
publisher

In December, 1996, after the article appeared in <u>Cinefex</u>, I received this letter from the publisher, complimenting me on the work and looking forward to the next article that we had arranged (always a good sign for a freelance writer). Note that despite the proliferation of drafts and lengthy period from inception to publication, the process was viewed as a necessary part of the re-writing continuum inherent to the best examples of written work. Though the editor and the publisher himself amended my corrected drafts, the final version which appeared was appreciated by everyone, the subject included. Future articles of mine would undergo similar steps and follow the basic course that all writers must take throughout their freelance careers. Even if there ends up being five, six, or ten drafts of your works, the published result – the only one that the public is going to read - is the one that truly counts. It is my sincere advice to all freelance writers that you should nurture, encourage, and embrace this creative process.

Chapter Seven

MARKETING YOUR MATERIAL

Utilizing the concept of "free" publicity

The concept of capitalism aside, how and why do magazines stay in business? Publicity. Is it free? Well, not exactly. Realizing the value of promoting their artists and projects (both current and "library" or older material), movie studios, TV networks, record companies, sports leagues, and other entertainment-based companies spend a significant amount of time, energy and money to ensure that their most vital material is in the public consciousness. They can do this through advertising, but that is extremely costly in every manner - to create and air a TV commercial or buy space in magazines and news-papers can often constitute a disproportionate amount of a project's entire budget. The answer? Publicity. The phrase "you can't buy that kind of publicity" is rooted in truth. By making their clientele available to the entertainment media, productions and companies get maximum exposure without having to pay out the hefty costs of advertising. How? Magazines need to fill pages. Readers want to know about their favorite artists, films, albums, teams, etc. By filling the blank pages of magazines and empty minutes of TV talk shows and entertainment news reports, projects and personalities capture that public attention which will ultimately push along their work. This is where you fit into the matrix of publicity:

A win-win-win situation

With publications needing to fill pages and artists demanding exposure, the freelance entertainment writer is in a comfortable position - you are needed on both ends. When you pitch an article that features a specific project to a widely read publication, three things are set in motion. First, the magazine now has a story about a

77

prominent person/project that will increase its sales. Second, the project or person in question has that always-important public exposure. Third, the freelance writer is now attached to the publication and client, facilitating that exposure. Hence, a win-win-win scenario develops.

The ongoing demand for stories and exposure

It is never-ending - week after week, month after month, year after year, a continuing publication must fill pages. Successful magazines need to maintain sales at their target level, increasing where they can, but keeping that steady flow of advertising capital coming in. Therefore, they need stories that are going to reliably pique their audience's interest. Most niche magazines have a built-in stable readership, and most of those publications are not oriented around "hot" celebrities. This is a positive for the freelance writer, since there are usually a consistent supply of available stories at this level from which you can viably choose a project. The higher-profile consumer publications are in constant, often vicious competition to profile the hottest celebrities and projects. Fortunately (or unfortunately, depending on your personal bent), these assignments are very rarely freelance-based, and if you happen to land one of them, you will not likely be a freelancer for long in the publishing world - someone is going to hire you as a staff writer in a hurry!

The necessity of intermediaries

If only it were as simple as pitching a story, getting a "green light" from a magazine, and interviewing your subject without interference. Well, remember how publicity was "not exactly free"? A healthy percentage of athletes, movie directors, actors, musicians and other personalities have representation with which you must communicate. This group consists of various handlers: agents, managers, business reps, publicists, or attorneys. Of the bunch, the publicist is the most likely candidate who will make your acquaintance at some point in the process (more on them a bit later). For the rest of the list, your strategy for reaching your desired interview subject will depend on several factors, one of them being your ability to write clearly-stated letters and faxes (a benefit!), but never lose sight of the ultimate goal: to reach your subject for an interview. If you maneuver through the network of "handlers" and reach your subject, the connections that you make may prove vital once your article is successfully published and you are on to other assignments.

PUBLICATIONS

Grasping the entertainment media

As we enter the 21st century, there are undoubtedly more freelance entertainment writing opportunities than ever before. With the proliferation of independent media productions, the diversification of cable TV, and the foreseeably exponential expansion of the Internet, the future looks brighter than ever to develop one's career as a freelance writer. At the end of this section, I will examine the other writing outlets available to freelancers; however, the focal point of developing one's freelance career remains publications.

Understanding the market

All are not created equally. For any two publications, there are two sets of aesthetics, two ways of setting deadline times, two levels of intensity, you name it. All of them are just simply different. As a freelance writer, when you receive one set of expectations from one magazine, you can be sure that they won't apply to the next one. Early in my career, I started writing for a magazine that was very picky about many technical aspects of my writing (I assume that a similar situation existed for their other freelance contributors). When I began to branch out and freelanced for other publications, I was shocked to realize that the particulars to which I was held for that first one no longer came into play. Of course, the writing ethics of that first pub-

79

lication were first-rate and stayed with me to some extent, but nearly all of the other publications for which I ended up writing were not nearly as insistent on particular stylistic writing points. You will find, unlike my initial experiences, that most entertainment media settle for good clean work and do not demand lofty standards of excellence. If you are coming from a strong collegiate background, be prepared to face most of your challenges from within. The broadly based con-sumer entertainment publications (for whom you are least likely to freelance) no doubt have some good writers, but they rarely get past the least common denominator. But again, no two are alike, and no two of your experiences will be exactly the same.

Quarterlies, monthlies, and weeklies

Periodical sounds like a reasonable word, yes? Yet for most publications, the word stands for pressure. A publication, whether a 100% freelance written bi-monthly or a completely staff (or in-house) written trade weekly, must produce issues on a regular basis. This means nearly round-the-clock stress-filled work to guarantee that an issue will be out in stores and on newsstands when it is promised to the public. A quarterly, for obvious reasons, has it easiest. Naturally, this type of publication has more time with which to nurture and supervise an issue, making sure that their quality level is high. Plus, their current issue can sit on the shelves for three months before a new one mandates that retailers send the old ones back for reimbursement, meaning that a quarterly has a longer chance to sell. A monthly or bi-monthly has relatively less time to tweak an issue, and must rapidly generate new material. By the time one issue is out there, rest assured that the next one is probably nearing completion. A weekly (or a daily, bless them!) has no time to play around. With a closed circle of known freelancers, these publications can probably scoot by, but it is a safe bet, with their insane schedules, that weeklies - and especially dailies - have full-time staff writers cranking out articles, editing them, shipping them off for layout, and moving on to the next piece, often within one issue's time.

The Big Pitch

So with the understanding that all publications are separate entities unto themselves, the freelance writer gauges the market and attempts the pitch. In doing so, a careful assessment of your target publication is in order. You will be working with the entire range of freelance opportunities, from the regimented trade journal that knows exactly what it wants in each issue, to the open broader-based magazine that accepts new ideas. The freelance writer must be a combination of things in this respect - attuned to what is currently happening in the select field, understanding of a publication's wants and needs, and aware of how to package his idea into an attractive selection for a publication. In doing so, the writer pitches his idea, suiting it to the specific publication.

In essence, as it pertains to freelance writers, a pitch is just a personal idea for a writing assignment that you present to a publisher. Pitches can be verbal or written, depending on your strengths. They should always be clear, as brief as possible, and not out of bounds with what you are capable of developing as a writer. Sometimes, pitches will work wonders, and other times you will just be spinning your wheels. Does the publication need your idea? Will it work? Is the timing right? Can you get the interview(s) that will be required to create that article? Will the piece be visual and, if so, is art (photos, graphics, imagery) available? You must answer all of these questions in advance if you want a magazine to seriously consider your pitch. This holds doubly true (or worse) if you have never before pitched a story idea to the publication in question. Have your article idea carefully planned out. Develop your written or verbal pitch. Try it out on friends or colleagues. Hone and rehearse. Then muster your confidence and approach the publication with your idea. Typically, unless the outlet in question is a completely closed shop, the publisher or editor will likely entertain your pitch. Then the answers to the above questions will determine the fate of your pitch.

My favorite personal pitch story involves an article I wrote for MovieMaker magazine. Its genesis and result may shed light on the pitching process and its potential outcome for freelance writers. I discovered, about a month before their deadline, that MovieMaker, for whom I had written several short freelance articles, was preparing a screenwriting issue. Having flirted with the screenwriting world myself, and not as yet having written about screenwriters per se, I quickly made it my mission to get an assignment for the issue. None were available.

Not discouraged, I racked my brain and came up with a great story idea - profiling a married couple, each of whom is a notable screenwriter in his/her own right, and neither of whom have been overexposed in the press. Plus, I had a previous personal connection to one of them, making the job of first contact much easier. The publisher approved the idea, I established contact, but I was soon disappointed to learn just why this couple had not been overexposed in the entertainment media: they flatly refuse such interviews. I was nearly resigned to being left out of the issue altogether. In desperation, I pitched a few other ideas, none of which were clicking, and with only two weeks before the issue's deadline, it seemed hope was lost.

The next day, a pleasant Sunday morning, I took a lengthy run around my neighborhood with the hopes of stirring some last-ditch idea that might yet be suitable for the issue (I generate an uncanny number of ideas when I exercise). By the time I reached my home, I had it: I would write about the influence of digital effects technology (which I had previously covered in a different capacity) on the screenwriting process, and I would interview three or four screenwriters — still do-able with a week to go — about the situation. The publisher loved it, we agreed on a 3000-word limit, and off I went into the afternoon. All that remained was to determine whom I would try to interview, what my angle would be, and how to put it all together - in 7 days! The next morning, via a concise fax that I had written to express my goals with the article, I put feelers out to nine screenwriters who had writ-ten movies that featured digital special effects within the previous 18 months. By Thursday of that week, I started my interviews, eventually getting phone time with seven of my targeted screenwriters. I spent two or three days transcribing my material, editing the quotes into useable material, and started writing. I got a crucial three-day extension to my deadline, did lots of original writing, integrated relevant quotes from each interview, and 11 days after conceiving the idea, had an article put to bed. Six weeks later, it was on newsstands, with a handsome photo spread that I helped to organize through the publicists of the said screenwriters' various production companies. In addition to my input and skills as a freelance writer, the realization of the article was a combination of a fresh approach to a current subject, accessible interview candidates, and a publisher who was willing to consider unsolicited pitches. It all worked in my favor in that case.

Busting the Catch-22

How are you going to get into the entertainment media without experience, and how do you get experience if you can't get in? This is a century-old problem for new talent of all extractions, but for the freelance writer, there are some specific things to consider that may ease the pain involved:

A. The reality of the business

How hard is it for a newcomer to break into the entertainment business and why? Picture this: on a pastoral weekend afternoon, you stroll through a large park. Several groups of people engage in idle activities. The company softball game takes place in one area, and children cut loose at the playground. On grassy stretches of the park, several families picnic on large blankets, sharing food and good times, casually minding their own business. How difficult would it be for you to approach one of the picnic blankets, sit down, and join the picnic? Now, how hard would it be to join on a regular basis, let's say every Saturday? Think of it this way: the picnicing family is the entertainment business. Could you join them? Not until they devoutly trusted you. They might give you some food or drink and send you on your way. Do they particularly want to hear why you want to join their picnic? Not really, and to join them on a long term basis would mean equal amounts of patience, persistence, and decent manners on your part, during which your covert goal of joining them for you own needs must remain your secret. To the family, you want to join because you like them and want to be part of their family! That holds universally true unless you have an immediately obvious reason why they should take you in without scrutiny. This is the reality of breaking into the entertainment business. It is a typically nepotistic closed shop which is historically wary of outsiders, and hopeful writers must have luck, timing, and talent on their side to maximize opportunities when they arise.

How complicated is it for a writer to initiate an idea in the entertainment business? The passage from idea to project is specific to movies, television, and live productions, but the basic path can probably be applied to other media as well. Picture this: a 12-story building where the top floor houses the lonely company executive in charge of production who "green lights" (or says 'yes' to) a mere handful of projects per year. If he okays more than his targeted amount, no matter how good the idea for that new show sounds, he runs the risk of spreading his resources too thinly for those projects he has already agreed to produce. So you enter his building in the lobby level. On each succeeding upward floor, a new member of the company's key production staff - already consumed with projects that have been put into motion - must be convinced that your idea is worth turning into yet another company production. If they are convinced, you get to go up one floor. If after the first 11, you have all "yes's" to your idea, you must inevitably face that lonely guy on level 12. Sure he's well-paid and in possession of perceived power, but he is also in danger of losing that job if his upcoming slate of productions fails to deliver consistent hits. For decades and decades, even largely successful executives of this kind have been dismissed from companies when their current track record begins to decline. "What have you done for me lately?" is the name of this game. Your scant hope of reaching level 12 to begin with is much improved if you can "attach" someone to your project - an actor, director, or other branch of talent who makes the 12th floor a more appealing possibility to everyone involved. If you can do so, a project has been ignited. When you are a trusted freelance writer for entertainment publications, your chances of direct involvement in projects that *do* get off the ground are greatly enhanced over those of would-be screenwriters and directors trying to get to level 12.

How hard is it for a new project to get off of the ground in the entertainment business? Picture this: clear our original park of families, children, and softball players. In their place, insert the twenty key people it takes to create a project such as a new TV show, movie, recording, live concert, etc. Let's assume that the artists involved are not complete newcomers (they have that crucial track record) and the other players are all seasoned (to some extent) at their various positions: company executives, the project's producer and/or director, casting or artists-and-repertoire personnel, narrative writer or songwriters, designers, etc. These folks don't even include the technical support people - crucial to the success, if not the launching of a project - who include cinematographers, costumers, makeup supervisors, engineers, set builders, etc. Back to our park. All of the "keys" or "principals" in our project are standing around various parts of the park, each with a piece of jigsaw puzzle in his/her hands. The idea is that everyone must come together at the same time in the precise position needed to create the completed puzzle. If they do so, your project gets off of the ground. If one person is missing when everyone manages to join together, or if some people are standing in the wrong position, the project does not go forward. After several failed tries at joining together, some of our principals will grow impatient and start leaving the park with their jigsaw piece in hand. If they can be quickly replaced, we try to create the finished puzzle again. If they cannot, we stall again, until finally most of the people abandon the attempt and head off to some other park. Usually the last person left in the park after a project has collapsed is the very first principal who took interest in the project - a producer or executive who was trying to shepherd

85

the project along. This is the reality of making a mainstream movie, album, TV show, etc. As a writer, having knowledge of this process is important when covering a project; your appreciation for and understanding of skilled craftsmanship within such a chaotic business will certainly improve as you become increasingly sensitive to the plight of the different artists who regularly work in Hollywood.

B. The freelance advantage

With your knowledge of how the business works, there are ways for you to overcome the catch-22 that pervades the entertainment media. Above all, remember that you are dancing on the fringes of the industry, nearly invisible when it comes to aforementioned mainstream productions. You can certainly become involved and known to principals involved in these productions, but your role is neither threatening nor encroaching: these projects are going to get made with or without you! Due to my role, at this point, I am on a first-name basis with many talented individuals with whom I never would have dreamed I would have a working relationship. Many of them are quite simply talented craftspeople who work whenever they can find a good project. Ironically enough, most of the people you will encounter - actors, writers, producers, directors, musicians, technical people - all work on a freelance basis themselves! Aside from contracted artists and technicians for most of these folks, when one project ends, are on their own in search of the next one. This does not apply to top-of-the-line talent, the performers and project supervisors who are so successful they are sought out by productions. And, unlike you, most of your interview subjects have an agent, manager, publicist, etc., who fields offers and strategically handles their career. But essentially, the free-lance basis on which many entertainment industry personnel conduct their affairs means that they will usually be glad to talk to you and promote their work. They often need you as much as you need them!

C. Gaining publications' trust

The essence of developing a relationship with a publication is not radically different from working with any boss that you might have: you must earn their trust and respect. Being a freelancer has its certain benefits in this area; you can make your own hours and work without someone looking over your shoulder. But your individual work methods should not dictate how you conduct your affairs with publications. A deadline is a deadline, period. You may certainly request an extension and work with a publisher in creating the deadline, but be sure to communicate these things in advance. If you are responsible and serious about your writing, you will not be making more work for the publisher than is absolutely necessary. Hand your work in on time, make sure it is presented as cleanly as possible, and show your dedication to the craft. This sounds amazingly simple, but you would be surprised by the tales I have heard from publishers who don't even receive that much commitment from writers. The basic perks of freelance writing, including the increasing prominence of your articles, the introduction of being assigned prestigious stories, and the confidence you receive from publishers, are the direct result of your prioritizing your relationships with publications. I've often been told by my publishers, "you're a real pro," and not understood what that meant. I didn't wake up one day in the middle of my career and decide to transform into a professional writer. Over time, I realized that the insinuation of their statement is that I am passionate, reliable, and dedicated to what I am doing. For any more information, please refer to the introduction of this book.

Alternatives in the new millennium

Over the past 10 years, many avenues have opened up for freelance writers, and this will undoubtedly continue well into the 21st century. In my own career, several such alternatives have presented themselves and led to entirely new strands of writing and publishing.

The World Wide Web

The Internet is still in its infancy. In the spring of 1994, an institution where I taught basic-level writing allowed access to various newsgroups on the Internet and the use of e-mail. Without reading the inches-thick manual, I toyed around on my bare bones workstation, and within a few weeks, I discovered how to read a newsgroup article, highlight text, and respond to a person's opinions. What instantly hit me is the vast world of writing and communicating opportunities that lay before me. I was conversing in the written form with people from not only across the U.S., but also with people from Europe, Asia, Australia, and even Africa. This was in the days before widely available graphics browsers (anyone remember Mosaic?), but the words were flowing, ideas were being exchanged, and remote contacts were being cemented. I developed ongoing "electronic friendships" with this new tool, even exchanging post-mail items with several contacts based on similar entertainment tastes. With the late 1990s popularity of the Web, with its beautiful audio-visual interfacing, a second world evolved, one that perhaps relied less on written exchanges, but with increasing access to e-mail, more users were able foster written relationships than ever before. While the art of handwriting letters is dying, a new reliance on written communications has created a wellspring of activity. It is into this new world that freelance writers must journey to gain unprecedented occasions to use their skills in a productive manner. Writing for Web-only publications is certainly in our near future.

In 1997, I began an e-mail relationship with the publisher of an on-line magazine called *Visual Effects Headquarters* (now solely available as an archive at www.vfxhq.com). The intricately designed site served as a regular provider of information and reviews of visual effects in current movies, TV shows, commercials, video games, and other outlets. Colorful and graphics driven, with ample imagery from the projects themselves, articles were strikingly presented with white text on black backgrounds. Through steady e-mails, I offered to write an article based on several interviews I had done with computer graphics animators who were once pioneers of stop-motion animation. The e-publisher had many of the photos already available on disk, and we developed and "published" the article in May of that year. With my e-mail address printed on the tail of the article, I received much response from it, mostly from people who wanted more information about the subject. I was happy to oblige and I considered it a positive first experience.

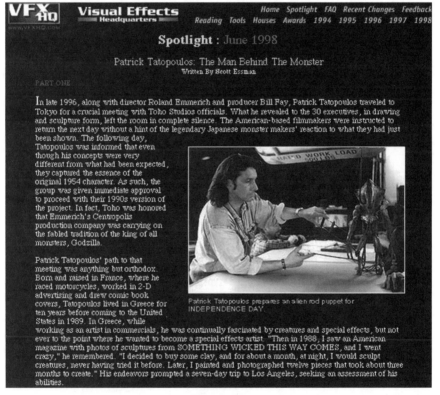

This article about *Godzilla's* creature designer, Patrick Tatopoulos, was among the first that the author published on the Internet, now a viable outlet for freelance writers.

The next spring, I approached the creator (publisher, shall we say) of the site with a new idea. At that time, through some industry connections, I had interviewed and visited a special effects designer/creator of characters, Patrick Tatopoulos, on the set of his latest project, *Godzilla*. Patrick had created various live-action scales of the creature which were supplemented on screen by a computer-generated version. Already preoccupied with another project for <u>Cinefex</u>, I was unable to publish my interview with Patrick in any larger context article about the film for that magazine. Thus, I pitched *Visual Effects Headquarters* on an article exclusively about Patrick. Although the article would not be a paid assignment, I knew that the guaranteed high-profile nature of summer 1998's *Godzilla* would mean a great deal of attention for my piece. The publisher and I agreed on a two-part article about Patrick: one involving his career prior to *Godzilla* and another strictly about his work on that film. I developed it, worked with Patrick's office in locating some great photos for the two sections, and they were published in June and July of 1998. I had no idea at that time exactly what their appearance was going to mean to my career.

International publishing

How viable is it, in this global age, to publish internationally? Well, after my two-part Patrick Tatopoulos article came out in June and July of 1998 on the Internet site, *Visual Effects Headquarters*, I received many e-mails from various parties interested in my attachment to Patrick's nascent career. Among them was an inquiry from a fan in France who edited a magazine called <u>L'Ecran Fantastique</u>. He wanted to know if I was interested in having my articles about Patrick translated into French and published in his magazine. Of course I was interested! It was a chance to have my work go international and reach a whole new audience. That in itself is a good reason to branch out, but on top of everything, <u>L'Ecran Fantastique </u> began to make me additional offers, eventually bestowing upon me the title of U.S. correspondent. Six months after their first inquiry, I was writing reviews, pitching original articles, and receiving major article assignments from them. I even developed a French-subtitled version of one of my video documentaries and had them advertise it for me. And yes, all of these have been paid ventures. Hence, with the ease of sending material through e-mail — either tied to the Internet or through another means — international publication is now a viable and legitimate outlet for freelance writers.

The concept of self-publishing

Should you run aground in attempting to expand your freelance writing boundaries, another option looms in the distance, one with considerably greater risk and more uncertain returns, but one which offers you complete control and unlimited autonomy: self-publishing. While the methods of doing so will be discussed later (see Chapter 9), the variety of choices which self-publishing offers makes it an appealing endeavor to those who must have their own forum in which to present their true voice. I had been writing for five different magazines, had created three video documentaries, and had produced three special live performances over a five-year period when I decided to launch my own publication, Directed By: The Cinema Quarterly, a periodical dedicated to interviews and analyses of film directors and their craft. After a year of planning and research, and nine months of intensive study about the field, Directed By debuted in October, 1998, with a cover story about director Bryan Singer. Despite the many pitfalls and setbacks, a self-published work has rewards which are unavailable from the large majority of most freelance writing assignments. To undertake the task involves undue amounts of self-sacrifice and long-term commitment, but I feel it is well worth the effort and fits with my overall sense of dedication and passion.

PUBLICISTS

A practical definition

Publicists, as much as any other group in the entertainment media, come in all shapes, sizes, and extractions, and can wield influence on the work of freelance writers perhaps more than anyone else in the field. Publicist, by the very term, are tasked with providing their client(s) with the proper exposure in the appropriate outlets, including print, broadcast, electronic, and other forms of publicity. They deal with publications, TV newsmagazines, talk show hosts, special promotional events, and, yes, writers. They do not subscribe to the adage "there's no such thing as bad publicity" (whether it is true or not), as they continually search for the best way to make their clients look worthy of attention in the vast public forum called the media. The perception that publicists are all rah-rah and upbeat is misleading, as you will find that many are thoughtful and care as much about their subject as you - like writers, it is their job to be passionate.

Some publicists are hired directly by a production company for a specific project, be it an album, tour, movie release, TV pilot, or other individual venture. This group works by-and-large on a freelance basis and is usually bouncing from project to project. The other main type of publicist is one working in an agency. The agencies, usually public-relations or specialty firms, are hired by individuals in the entertainment industry who want to a) generate more publicity for themselves, or b) want a liaison between themselves and the press at large. In either case, a specific in-house publicist will be assigned to the client and is expected to get his name, image, and abilities known to as many outlets as possible. They deal directly with publications, facilitating stories about their clients, providing support materials, and helping to keep the information flowing on a continuing basis.

With that in mind, it is a very good idea to maintain friendly, mutually respectful relationships with publicists. Make first contact with publicists, describing your work and the relationships that you have with different publications. Discuss story ideas together - make them part of the process. With some of your desired interview subjects, you may be able to directly contact them at their office or on the site of a production. In that case, you may not need to work with or even contact a publicist. Not everyone in the entertainment media has contracted the services of a publicist, and if you catch your subject between projects, you are likely to circumvent the need for dealing with a publicist. But most of the time, especially if the project is in progress or has just been released, your interview requests will be steered in the direction of the publicist assigned to the project. Treat them well and you will likely receive many useful resources.

The benefit of your publicist

In an ideal world, every freelance writer would have a publicist to do all of the work that one must do before sitting down to conduct an interview for one's article. The best publicists use their energies to assist you in determining who you should interview, help to schedule and arrange interviews, brief the subjects on the nature of the intended publication, write and send faxes accordingly, acquire useful background materials - including resumes and production notes about your project - and compile photoimagery useful to your piece. If you require special visitations or personal meetings with subjects (perhaps to witness specific parts of the project while it is being created), the publicist is your ticket to getting there.

That said, be sure to evaluate the temperament of your publicist. As with any group of people on whom you must rely, understand who you are dealing with and how far you can go with them. Many publicists are wonderfully outgoing and eager to help. One summer day, early in an assignment to write about a big studio movie, I was once invited to a big Disney press party and set visitation without first contacting the publicist on the project. Quite simply, she was informed that I was writing about the movie for a specific publication, and she sought me out! On this film, the publicist was so dutiful that she asked me back to the set some months later when she realized that a particular series of effects shots were being done that were central to my story. I have had many similar experiences with other publicists.

Be warned that the other side to this coin is the publicist who does not personally seek you out and is displeased about your sudden appearance in his project. On two different occasions in one six-month stretch (one was a TV show and another was a movie, both very big-budget main-stream projects), I had spent weeks negotiating to arrive on the set. In each case, the purpose of the visit was to observe activity crucial to a video documentary that I was creating (though it did not involve bringing a camera to the set). I had received the proper clearances to arrive at the location - in the first case from the legal department, and in the latter, from the director of the film. But, for various reasons, when I got there, the publicists went on the offensive against me. It did not seem to me that I was bothering anyone or overstaying my welcome in either of these cases, but neither publicist was open to my remaining on his set for my planned observations. I was verbally abused, nearly threatened, and my relationship with the initial contact that got me on to those projects was tainted as a result. In my heart, I knew I was doing nothing wrong, and I also knew that long after those publicists had gone on to other things, I would still be struggling to realize my project. The lesson to learn here is to be careful - not every publicist will understand your importance as a writer, and you will not always be treated appropriately. Regardless of whether these bad experiences are commonplace or exceptional, it is better to be wise and gauge your publicist's predisposition to helping you in your quest for an article, and always use that knowledge to act accordingly. It may save you some unnecessary grief during your travels.

Working in tandem

Surely the best possible situation is when your publicist works with you! As in the case of the publicist inviting me to the set, project-based publicists can be an enormous help to you. In the case of agency-based publicists, those less tied down to one particular project, here are some pointers on working together:

Client lists

Often, an agency with which you are interacting will have a storehouse of clients who could be integral to you in a current article or in developing new article ideas. I was once referred to a publicity firm by a magazine for which I had written several articles. I interviewed one client, an author, about a biography he had written, and it went so well the publicist offered several other clients to me. The others worked in capacities that were related to the client who constituted my original assignment. This evolution led to two additional articles for the same publication, and a new article for a second publication! It was a good example of networking within an agency and working in tandem with a publicist.

Offer - do not ask!

Remember that the job of the entertainment publicist is to get all of his clients (in this case, in an agency) positive exposure in the media. But you are only one writer with, ideally, a close group of publications for which you freelance. Therefore, it is impossible for you to take on the entire clientele of a specific agency. Your job, instead, is to establish a mutually advantageous relationship with the agency; then, having a knowledge base of their clients, offer specific ways in which you could develop and pitch new article ideas about select clients to publications. In this way, you are offering publicity to them, and you will likely get all of the help you need. Working with one agency for the first time on one article, I used their clientele list to initiate additional articles about George Lucas' biographer and the chairman of the newly active RKO Radio Pictures studio. Through a liaison with a different agent at that same firm, I later created a feature article about production designers in cinema for <u>MovieMaker</u>. I did not have to ask for their help, for I endeavored to offer them a unique method of publicity instead. It led to four articles!

Opening 2-way communications

This cannot be stressed enough: working with publicity is all about communication. Granted, in my bad experiences with publicists, even open communication might not have thwarted the negative treatment

I received, but I will say this: I could not have had the good experiences that have come my way without the fluid back-and-forth contact between the publicists and myself. If the phone is not your friend (see Chapter 3, Section B), generate your communication through fax, e-mail, or old-fashioned post-mail letter writing. But rest assured that your position with publicists will improve in direct correlation to the manner and frequency with which you communicate with them.

All *Wizard of Oz* tribute photographs by Deverill Weekes

This is <u>not</u> a scene from the movie! Look closely - this is actually a moment from the author's 1998 tribute to *The Wizard of Oz*, to mark the 60th anniversary of the making of that classic MGM film. Producing innovative projects such as this one is one way a freelance writer can expand his or her career.

Chapter Eight

EXPANDING YOUR BOUNDARIES

Assuming that you have forged your way as a freelance writer and established yourself as a reliable source of professional journalism, you may wish to diversify by generating new types of media projects. Since a freelance writer might face obstacles when taking "normal routes" towards developing his career, one obvious path towards breaking down barriers is producing original projects that attract attention and establish you within the entertainment community. My choice for venturing beyond the boundaries of standard writing assignments was to produce my own video documentaries. While that does not necessarily mean that *you* should devote years of your life travelling the world to pursue an obscure performer from the early years of vaudeville — though there is nothing wrong with that — making short-form videos about familiar material is a viable enterprise for passionate writers. If you have been regularly covering one particular field and know your subject matter well enough, making a documentary can be a natural extension of your professional endeavors and a way to garner further reknown as an authority in your field. While I am a fan of all types of documentaries, covering Hollywood subjects gave me an extra incentive to move into documentary media: what better way to further engross myself in the worlds of makeup artists and special effects people? With that in mind, I set about to visually capture Hollywood artists and craftspeople at their work. At the same time, I put my subjects onto videotape, much like I had done in committing my observations and interviews to writing. Without question, over the past five years, all of my special projects infused my writing career with new life – both my documentaries and the events on which they were based promoted my reputation in this field and created a host of new writing opportunities for me. At some point in your own career, you may find a need to develop ancillary personal projects. What follows here is a detailed description of my documentary efforts with the hope that it inspires you in some fashion to push the envelope and broaden your own Hollywood base.

Finding a Documentary Subject

Obviously, when you set out to create a documentary of any kind, you must ideally have an upcoming event or ongoing subject in your selected field of interest available for coverage. In the Hollywood media, the best opportunities for documentary subjects are essentially the same as for freelance writing purposes: productions of major entertainment projects. The preparation and creation of a film, album, TV show, theatrical production, radio or TV broadcast, live performance, awards show, special promotional event or sporting event all offer optimal venues for documenting the various crafts necessary to realize those projects. As I described in chapters 2 and 3, however, another catch-22 will surface as you pursue more high-profile projects. For example, even after I had cemented my reputation for thoroughly covering Hollywood projects (albeit in print, not on video or film), I was regularly bypassed in my attempt to cover similar (or in some cases the same) projects as a behind-the-scenes documentarian. It is simple economics: the bigger a project gets, the more people will be swirling around that project, trying to "attach" themselves to it.

Most major Hollywood projects, in fact, have pre-packaged deals with independent documentary producers to create "EPKs," or electronic press kits. With a combination of interviews, backstage footage, and in-production action, EPKs are often used by the company producing the film, album, or event in question as promotional devices for entertainment news TV shows, such as *Entertainment Tonight*, *Access Hollywood*, *Extra*, and *E! News Daily*. Often, an EPK will also air on cable or syndicated channels when a project is ready to debut, and some of them wind up as separate rental/sales items, either as "The Making of XXX" or on a separate track of a DVD (or special video reissue of a movie for an anniversary). On several occasions, I was considered for EPK movie assignments but lost out to other producers who already had been doing them for the studio or production company involved in the film. It's a safe bet that the documentary for the next big DreamWorks movie has been promised to the producer of the doc made for *American Beauty*. No matter how interesting your documentary idea may be, DreamWorks will likely not even consider such a proposal from a total outsider. Nonetheless, there are several alternatives to trying to latch on to a major project in order to complete a documentary, and I pass on some reasonable avenues you might consider taking.

Independent Entertainment Projects

If major Hollywood productions are off-limits to you, making documentaries about smaller projects is certainly a more realistic proposition. For every big-budget studio movie, recording, live performance and TV program in existence, there are dozens of independently produced efforts that are being assembled all over the world. Often, these projects are off of the Hollywood radar and ignored until they prove themselves by performing in the marketplace. These projects are ripe fodder for any freelancer aspiring to branch out into documentary production. Though the low-profile nature of these projects makes them easy to dismiss for potential journalists, there are several reasons why you, as a nascent writer-producer, should seriously consider covering independent entertainment projects:

1) You may catch onto a good wave
2) You will generate documentary material to showcase your skills
3) You will increase your overall surface area by networking with others involved in the project

In his perceptively accurate book <u>Adventures in the Screen Trade</u>, William Goldman noted that "nobody knows anything" in Hollywood, insinuating that each project is a crapshoot - success and failure are ultimately indeterminate. This holds true for all media projects, whether or not they qualify as legitimate "Hollywood." In

101

the past decade, who knew about the latent commercial potential of such films as *Clerks*, *The Crying Game*, *El Mariachi*, *Pulp Fiction*, and *The Blair Witch Project*, until buzz and film festivals made them household names? Who would have thought that Nirvana's *Nevermind*, Pearl Jam's *Ten*, and Alanis Morissette's *Jagged Little Pill* would all come out of obscurity to overturn the way that musical acts were signed and marketed? During their early lives, these projects – and all independent entertainment fare – exist under the media radar. Even though you might have had trouble pitching stories about those projects to publications before they were released, there is a good chance that you could have offered to cover those projects as a bystanding documentarian and met with little resistance. Easy to say now, but there are *El Mariachis* and *Neverminds* being produced somewhere every day – the challenge is to find these projects before the buzz has started.

In my case, by December of 1995, I was cold calling makeup studios in search of interviews, but was meeting some brick walls. One such obstacle, however, indirectly led to my first professional video documentary. When I called Cannom Creations to request an interview, I was thoroughly blocked, as described in detail earlier in this book. Yet all was not lost, even on that first call. When I first got through to the studio, I decided to describe my intentions to anyone who would listen (being green might have helped in this respect). Luckily, I found a willing listener in Todd Tucker, one of the key makeup/creature artists at Greg Cannom's shop, having worked on such groundbreaking films as Bram Stoker's *Dracula*, *Mrs. Doubtfire*, and *The Mask*. Todd informed me that it might be difficult to get Cannom to commit to an interview at that time, but that he himself was soon to be producing his own personal project, a creature-oriented fantasy film called *Wolvy*. He explained that there was nobody else documenting this production and he invited me to cover the project over the two-day shoot.

For the author's first documentary project, he covered the making of creature artist Todd Tucker's independent fantasy film *Wolvy*, later editing the footage into a 30-minute video.

After the success of the author's first documentary with Tucker, he was invited to cover the follow-up, another fantasy centered on the demonic character Luth (pictured) who rules *The Underworld*.

103

Though I had never before made a professional film, I sensed that documenting *Wolvy* was the ideal chance to do so. Plus, it was a wholly do-able process. Seizing the opportunity, I assembled a skeleton crew, arranged for the rental of equipment, then shot behind-the-scenes footage and interviews over the two days in February 1996. Five months later, after studying the footage and creating a detailed EDL (edit decision list), I entered a studio and cut two versions of my work: a two-minute music video-style behind-the-scenes piece and a 30-minute fully realized documentary video called *Making Wolvy*. While I have used the full-length version as a sale and promotional item to demonstrate my documentary skills, Tucker himself has used the two-minute tape to help pitch his project to potential video distribution outlets. Moreover, my material was shown to other makeup artists and studios around town, creating more demand for my work and wider respect for my abilities, both of which facilitated my future special events and documentaries. Thus, taking advantage of the door opened in front of me (almost disguised by one failed phone call!), I found my first documentary subject and turned it into an important facet of my career. You may find it noteworthy that I steadfastly maintained my relationship with Tucker, documenting his next project, *The Underworld*, and involving him in my future projects whenever I could.

Know Your Equipment

One clear benefit of being a documentary producer in the new millennium is having many options in one's choice of formats. While most documentaries in former decades were completed in 16mm film, video has been the name of the game in the past 25 years - 3/4" video was once a standard format; then consumer formats like Super VHS and Hi-8 became popular. For the best possible picture quality and the most user-friendly system in the editing room, Betacam SP is now the premiere choice. However, unless you have immediate access to a Betacam SP camera, renting one costs up to $300 per day, and that doesn't include mandatory accessories such as sound and lighting. Usually, you can make a deal with a rental house so that you check out the equipment on a Friday afternoon, return it on a Monday morning, and only pay for one day's rental fee. Prices of Betacam SP stock have dramatically come down in the past five years - whereas a 30-minute tape cost $25.50 in 1995, by 2000 the price had dropped to under $17. With Betacam SP, utilizing a proper shotgun microphone to back up high-quality lavaliere mikes (for interview segments), you will get excellent sound on your tapes with two tracks of audio. Also, consumer digital video has just been put on the market in the late 1990s. While not as sharp as Betacam, Mini-DV systems offer workable sound and picture in a relatively cost-effective system (list price of Sony's DV home camera/sound system was under $4000 at this printing). After shooting is completed, it is recommended that you transfer all of your Betacam SP or Mini-DV tapes to VHS format with a "window dub," that is, a transfer of your footage to a home-friendly system where you can view your shots with visible timecode on the screen. By using timecodes - the exact count numbers from 01:00:00:00 to 01:29:59:29 on a thirty minute tape, corresponding to the precise hour, minute, second, and frame (from 1 to 30) of each moment that you have shot - you will be able to pick your usable shots from among the many possibilities that your footage offers. If you spend time at home selecting shots and putting them into a cohesive sequence, the closer you can get to achieving a final EDL that will save you precious time in the editing room.

Working with Crews

Much like making a movie, an album, or a live performance, making a documentary is a collaborative effort. While you, as the writer-producer, have considerable creative and organizational responsibilities, you must ideally recruit a crew to handle technical aspects of your production. Those of you who are now wondering why you would want to leave the comfort of your office, where you and a word processing program are all that you need to succeed in a freelance writing career, may now wish to turn to Chapter 9! Yes, documentary efforts involve a great deal of work - in addition to researching, selecting, and financing equipment needs, you must have people who can operate the technology, not only competently, but with enough skill so that you will be proud to show your work to the Hollywood subjects whom you engage. However, the work will pay off and likely lead to more networking and writing opportunities as long as you create informed and technically proficient projects. While I had little trouble at mastering the art of recording interview audio onto a DAT recorder, shooting and recording a documentary on Betacam SP requires a more refined technical ability. Ideally, you must find crew members who are excited about the subject and can offer their skills in exchange for the experience. While searching local film schools can lead to finding qualified candidates, you are more apt to assemble a reliable crew by calling on acquaintances who you meet in your professional writing pursuits — don't be afraid to talk to crew members of film, TV and music projects and explain your limited financial situation. Often you will find that if technical personnel understand you are shooting your project on spec or for portfolio reasons, they will not demand financial compensation. If you properly feed and attend to your crews' aesthetic needs, you will keep them happy during the throes of production. You may even find a kindred spirit along the way who will gladly join you in future projects to shoot your footage, record your sound, or assist with lighting and grip. In my four professional documentary projects, I have been fortunate to work with similar crews, and in instances when they had to back out, individuals were happy to refer me to other collaborative technicians.

Editing Your Material

During the 1970s and 1980s, the life of video editors was a tough one. The linear concept of A/B roll editing — in which selected shots from different source tapes in the "A" videocassette deck would be put onto a master tape in the "B" deck — was incredibly time-consuming, imperfect, and worst of all, irreversible. Often, to fix a section in the middle of the master tape meant a great deal of doctoring, and to make major changes meant a total overhauling of the project. Then a miraculous thing happened. Seeded in the 1980s with systems such as Montage and Editdroid, non-linear editing was invented. Using a combined videotape-computer interface, digitized media could be selected, edited, and rearranged by a software program in any desirable order any number of times before being outputted to a final master tape. By the mid-1990s, nearly the entire film industry had converted to non-linear systems: Avid Film Composer became one of the industry standards. Although a team of film assistants must ultimately conform the computer version of an edited project to the original film negative, the process has certainly made the technical task of editing simpler. With video, one's digitized media - your master tapes on a project - is directly accessible in a non-linear system, and a master tape struck from an editing session is the final product from which you can make duplications. If it is at all possible, **gain access to a non-linear editing system to edit your material**. Typical editing systems rent for $100-$200 per day, not including the services of an editor who can operate the equipment, so you must be as prepared as possible before you go into an editing room. Due to curiosity, I used Avid, Media 100, and other systems to edit my 30-minute documentaries and linear systems to cut my shorter pieces: there is no contest! I strongly advise locating Avid or a similar system to cut your footage. Depending on the amount of material you wish to digitize into the system, you will need an according amount of storage - usually defined in gigabytes. When you consider that a CD holds 650 megabytes, a gig holds quite a bit of memory. Yet digitized video holds so much information, you will need at least 9 gigs, perhaps up to 32 gigs to cut a typical 30-minute documentary. If your EDL is pretty accurately timed out, you will have under 45 minutes of desired shots to include in your piece and can edit it down from there. While cutting 30 tight minutes might take weeks using a linear system, it can easily be reduced to days with a non-linear one. And don't forget that last-minute decision to move a shot from the middle of your program to the very end. In an Avid, you can do so, watch the new segment, and implement it or change it back, all within minutes. With all of my projects, as I will describe in greater detail in the next section of this chapter, my writing skills were the life-force of my video documentaries; I wrote the scripts for all of them, incorporating historical material with interview questions, voice-over, behind-the-scenes shots that I selected, and special stills that I inserted at key moments in the program. In fact, just recently, one of my favorite collaborators, Will Hooke, a writer-editor-cinematographer, told me that I was the most prepared writer-director with whom he had ever collaborated! In this way, I feel that my writing and documentary producing careers have become interchangeable.

Creating Your Own Events

One way I ensured that I was making documentaries about material that was important to my career was in developing, then document-ing, my own special Hollywood events. I had achieved some success with *Making Wolvy* in late 1996, but what I really wanted was to cre-ate the ultimate documentary about makeup people, one that would feature many of them together in one place, discussing their favorite projects and strongest influences. In numerous interviews, makeup people had repeatedly mentioned one name when discussing their strongest influences: Dick Smith. What better subject for a special event that would unite all of these artists than Dick Smith himself, the godfather of modern makeup who influenced a generation of young people who would go on to the forefront of Hollywood crafts? The idea eventually came to me that I should create a tribute to Smith, bringing everyone who I had interviewed together for one memorable event. After I was able to commit Smith to a lengthy phone interview about his career's work, I realized that he would be an excellent candidate for such a tribute. Though I initially caught him while he was in the midst of re-writing a professional makeup course that he frequently updates, when we finally sat down to talk, Smith gave me five hours of interview time, still the most that any one subject has ever given to me. We discussed his beginnings in makeup during the very first years of television in New York, his pioneering achievements in his numerous movie projects, and his continued rapport with young and upcoming artists. After all of those interview hours, I realized the importance of this man to his field and the degree to which he has touched others. Though this type of event was a risky proposition for a Hollywood newcomer, as a writer, I knew that it would at *least* provide me with rich documentary material and blaze new trails for possible writing subjects. By the summer of 1996, I was organizing my tribute in full.

Prior to his special tribute to Dick Smith, the author conducted an extensive career retrospective interview with Smith about the inner workings of all of his key projects, including *The Hunger*, in which he took David Bowie through five separate old-age stages of makeup.

In September of 1996, I hosted a surprise tribute to Smith, knowing that he would be coming to the Los Angeles area from his Florida home during one select weekend. Trusting my instincts, I quite simply rented a hotel ballroom, invited dozens of Smith's closest industry friends, and put together my documentary team. When I picked Smith up from his nearby hotel room, he had no idea what awaited him. Amusingly, the undisclosed irony was that I had no idea what I had in store that afternoon either.

Photo by Stanley Newton

For his 1996 tribute to Dick Smith, the author gathered together the makeup legend's peers, protégés and admirers in a celebration of his 50 years in the industry. Pictured are:

First row: Greg Nicotero, Robert Short, Bob Burns, Harry Thomas (deceased one month after photo was taken), Abe Haberman (deceased January, 1998)
Second row: Estelle Shay, Kevin Haney, Don Post, Jr., Bill Malone, Rick Baker, Dick Smith, Forrest Ackerman, Todd Tucker
Back row: Don Shay, Craig Reardon, Stuart Ziff, Kate Studley, Alec Gillis, Tom Woodruff, Jr.

I had decorated the reception room with posters of Smith's most noted films: *Little Big Man, The Godfather, The Exorcist, Taxi Driver, Altered States,* and *Amadeus,* for which he won the 1984 Academy Award. Through the two-hour main event, I called each of the attendees up to the speaking podium, allowing them to share thoughts and anecdotes about their experiences with Smith and the influence he had on them. Then I showed a 10-minute video that I produced which highlighted Smith's most notable film makeups. Lastly, I organized group interviews of Smith with various other guests, discussing Smith's influence in concert. Foremost among these segments was a 45-minute session with Dick and his closest protégés in attendance: Rick Baker, Kevin Haney, and Craig Reardon. Without the venue of the tribute, I **never** would have been able to organize this interview and the passions that it unearthed in the four subjects. Never had they been interviewed together in that way, and it was instrumental in bringing me close to future personal and professional projects with Smith, Baker, Reardon, and Haney. Most all of the footage from the day's proceedings - plus additional interview material I shot some months later with absentees - became the cornerstones for my 1998 30-minute documentary *A Tribute to Dick Smith*, which has been universally regarded as an important video project in the Hollywood makeup field. One other thing about that project: as I knew that there were many people who were unable to attend my tribute but who would have liked to participate, I suggested that they write letters to Smith which I could read aloud to the audience in their place. Among the industry people I contacted was George Lucas. Though I didn't know it then, he was in the middle of preparing the re-release of the original *Star Wars* trilogy, but through his publicist, I was informed that he would send me a letter for the tribute. Even among Hollywood's elite, the name of George Lucas, revealed at the conclusion of the letter, provoked a visible reaction in the audience. What's more, I prepared a framed photo of Smith from the tribute and was invited to Skywalker Ranch in Northern California to personally deliver it to Lucas (no, I did not get to meet the man, but the trip inside the famed ranch was worthwhile and broke the ice with the organization of yet another legendary Hollywood figure). Subsequently, I formed a liaison with Lucas' ILM effects facility and wrote about several of their projects, including *Mighty Joe Young, Men in Black*, and *Galaxy Quest*.

111

September 6, 1996

Mr. Dick Smith
c/o Mr. Scott Essman
P. O. Box 1722
Glendora, CA 91740

Dear Dick,

I'm so sorry that I am unable to attend your celebration. Please know how much I appreciate your extraordinary contributions to the art of special makeup effects. Everyone in the industry is indebted to you. Congratulations and best wishes!

Sincerely,

George Lucas

Though he was unable to attend the author's tribute to Dick Smith in person, George Lucas sent this personal letter which the author read aloud during the event.

In all, for roughly $1000 plus video post-production costs, my tribute to Dick Smith brought me a series of career opportunities and respect from my peers and subjects that would have been unthinkable beforehand. Needless to say, I ingratiated myself with a legendary Hollywood figure and showed the producers and publishers with whom I wished to work in the future that I was capable of originating my own successful projects. Most importantly, the tribute took my freelance writing career into new directions. Within months, my first published article appeared and I began to write for three additional magazines. As a result of the tribute's popularity, I gained invaluable exposure for my subsequent work.

A Second Tribute

Why settle for one special event when the concept had worked so well? In 1997, I chose to create a tribute (with accompanying video documentary) for another makeup legend of the same importance as Smith. While Dick Smith had established himself and succeeded on the East Coast, John Chambers did so on the West Coast, like Smith working in television (both were at NBC), moving to films in the early 1960s, and breaking important ground with *Planet of the Apes*. That was the film that made Chambers' name, started the careers of numerous young makeup artists, and revolutionized the use of prosthetics to create memorable screen characters. Chambers had begun work on *Apes* in January of 1967, so I had timed it well – we could create a 30th anniversary of the project. In addition to that, 1997 was the year of Chambers' 75th birthday. My tribute date was set when I noted that September 12 - his birthday - occurred on the same weekend of my Dick Smith tribute the year before. Coincidence or good karma?

For the author's tribute to John Chambers, actor Brian Peck lent this actual prop from the 1968 film, *Planet of the Apes*: the lawgiver statue was a nine-foot tall fiberglass giant that welcomed guests into the party.

Originally scheduled as a more intimate party, my Chambers tribute soon grew to twice the size of the one I had held for Smith, not due to any difference in their popularity, but because the word had gone out on the success of the first one. Soon I realized that the Chambers party was going to be a bigger deal in every sense. I was going to need more crew, more ambience, and some kind of special ingredient to show that I was up to the challenge of meeting the anticipation. Like the Smith tribute, I had posters, a compilation film, and many guest speakers, but where Smith has been quite active even since he stopped doing makeup on movies in 1987, Chambers had taken himself completely out of the business since his mid-1980s retirement.

As such, I felt as though we needed to punch up the sense of occasion - to make it into an all-inclusive birthday party, career tribute, and coming out celebration. Given that, I recruited as many members of the *Planet of the Apes* team as I could, getting the late Roddy McDowall, who had acted in many of the *Apes* films and TV shows that Chambers worked on – and was one of the nicest gentlemen I ever met in Hollywood - to give the keynote speech. Also, I wanted Chambers to see how much he had influenced and entertained contemporary Hollywood artists - even those he may not have known personally - by realizing his vision with *Apes*. After all, Chambers had been one of only two makeup men who received honorary Oscars for their work in movies when he got a statue for *Apes* in 1968 (the other being William Tuttle, who won a statue for *The Seven Faces of Dr. Lao* in 1964), as there was no regular category for makeup in the Academy Awards prior to 1981. But there was still one last missing item. We needed some Apes!

Brian Penikas and his group designed and produced nine character re-creations from *Planet of the Apes* for the author's surprise tribute to the creator of the original *Apes* makeup, John Chambers, on the occasion of his 75th birthday.

So, being a diligent freelance entertainment writer with another tribute in mind, I conducted a great deal of research to find out everything *Ape*. Who were those original artists whose careers started with that first 1967 *Apes* film? How could I gather them together for a group interview about the film? And who in Hollywood is an expert on the Ape characters themselves? Through noted makeup artist Jill Rockow, I had a reference to Brian Penikas and his troupe of performers/creature people called Apemania (a hybrid of *Planet of the Apes* and *Beatlemania*: "not the real apes, but an incredible simianulation!"). At first, I was hesitant to have my intimate event overrun by a bunch of masked men, but seeing Penikas and his work, I realized that they were a serious outfit - their makeups and costumes were perfect re-creations of the key figures from the Apes films (no Charlton Heston required), and the actors were all very excited about the concept of honoring John Chambers. Eventually, nine characters were slated for the tribute, and even I was shocked at the reaction to their unannounced entry to the party. Here were veteran Hollywood artisans, standing up, pointing, and cheering as if it were a sporting event at the sight of Chambers' recreated *Apes* characters. Undoubtedly, Apemania was a hit, and I made sure to prominently feature them in my post-party interviews and in my video documentary. Also, early that morning, I had astutely sent my documentary cameraman to the Apemania headquarters (called Makeup and Monsters studio) to get behind-the-scenes footage of the makeups being applied; this ensured that I had adequate coverage of their work when I eventually went to the video editing stage.

Once the apes had made their appearance, I had a pleasant surprise when Martin Landau showed up. As he had worked with Chambers on the *Mission: Impossible* TV series, I had sought his participation, contacted his agent and repeatedly faxed him invitations without a response. He told me that he hadn't called because he was unsure if he could make it, but it was a great moment for everyone present when Landau entered the room. Both he and McDowall spoke eloquently and fondly of their days with Chambers, and the reunion of the original *Apes* creative team was a warm unique moment for everyone at the scene. For all of these reasons combined, plus due to Chambers' sincerely appreciative reactions, I believe that this was the most successful of all of my special events, and it went on to become the best selling of all of my video documentaries.

"A TRIBUTE TO JOHN CHAMBERS"

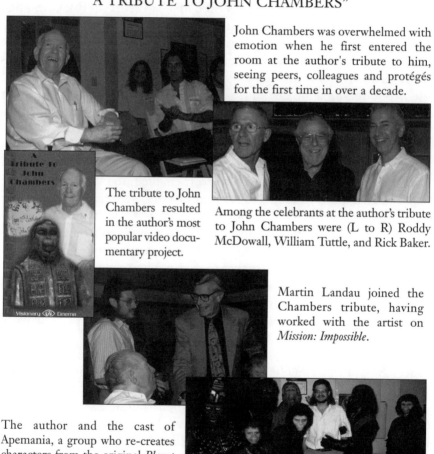

John Chambers was overwhelmed with emotion when he first entered the room at the author's tribute to him, seeing peers, colleagues and protégés for the first time in over a decade.

The tribute to John Chambers resulted in the author's most popular video documentary project.

Among the celebrants at the author's tribute to John Chambers were (L to R) Roddy McDowall, William Tuttle, and Rick Baker.

Martin Landau joined the Chambers tribute, having worked with the artist on *Mission: Impossible*.

The author and the cast of Apemania, a group who re-creates characters from the original *Planet of the Apes* film that brought John Chambers an honorary Oscar for makeup in 1968.

Photos by Bob Romero

116

Three is the Charm

Maybe it's superstition, but I think things work well in threes. Hence, after creating special live tributes and video documentaries for Dick Smith and John Chambers, I started planning a third event in early 1998. I suppose I was getting good at planning these tributes – they were virgin territory to everyone who attended them and created the right type of buzz for me: I was doing respectful quality work that paid tribute to the pioneers of Hollywood. Several attendees pointed out that I was blazing a new trail in their field, surprising for someone who was not himself a makeup artist. Still riding the wave from the Chambers event — I was now writing regularly for <u>Makeup Artist</u> Magazine —— I learned that the fall of 1938 was the starting point for production on *The Wizard of Oz*. This would make the fall of 1998 a proper choice for a timely tribute to the classic MGM film, which would probably garner even more attention than the other events I had produced. By this time, I had produced dozens of articles on makeup people, not to mention three 30-minute video documentaries and the two tributes. Knowing this, I sensed that we could accomplish something very special with regards to *Oz*. Many artists had told me that if I did another tribute, they would gladly be part of it and contribute makeups in the spirit of what Penikas and Apemania had accomplished for my Chambers tribute. However, getting a makeup person to commit to doing such intensive makeups, knowing that there was no budget, was an entirely different matter. Fortunately, in the early summer of 1998, Bill Corso, a brilliant young makeup supervisor, referred me to a friend of his, Jess Harnell, who was appearing in a local theatrical production of *The Wizard of Oz* which attempted to precisely simulate the characters from the film.

117

CENTER E   13
RESERVED
JUNE   26 1998

THE GROVE
THEATRE
UPLAND, CA

AT THE GROVE
PRODUCTIONS
PRESENTS

THE WIZARD
OF OZ

SIERRA Tickets, Monrovia, CA

FRIDAY 7 29 PM
JUNE   26 1998

ADMIT
ONE $17.00

CENTER E   13

Urged by his friend (and eventual *Oz* tribute makeup supervisor) Bill Corso, the author went to see a stage production of *The Wizard of Oz* from which several performers were selected to join the cast of the upcoming tributes to the film and its iconic characters.

After I went to see them perform, I was duly impressed with the cast (though I felt the makeups needed work), and after the show, I got many of them interested in doing my tribute. Bill and his handpicked team would create makeups for the "good" characters - Dorothy, the Scarecrow, the Tin Man, and the Cowardly Lion; their costumes came courtesy of the Grove Theater in which I met the actors. Matthew Mungle, another prominent makeup artist, had created a beautiful Wicked Witch and Flying Monkey for an Energizer Bunny TV commercial, and both he and those performers were game to join the fun. For the Witch's domineering Winkie Guard, I chose my friend Todd Tucker to create an original makeup for a 6'7" actor he had used in his *Underworld* project, and costume designer Jennifer McManus, who I would call upon later, created the Winkie Costume from scratch, easily the most complicated design from the original film. Referencing my past successes, I selected the second Saturday in September, 1998 as the date of my 60th anniversary event, and we set about to create an environment suitable to honoring a true American classic: I located a giant Emerald City backdrop, chose special theatrical lights, recruited a documentary crew, including a special sound man who wireless-miked the performers, and brought in a musician who had accompanied the actors for the earlier stage version. We would keep all of this a complete surprise from our invited industry audience, who had surely come to see us outdo the *Ape* achievements from the now-famous Chambers tribute.

118

Original Munchkin Jerry Maren with the author's tribute to *The Wizard of Oz*: Jeanne Castagnaro as Dorothy, Ken DeShan as the Scarecrow, Bob Stilwell as the Tin Man, Jess Harnell as the Cowardly Lion, Denise Moses as the Wicked Witch, Joe Griffo as the Flying Monkey, and Rob Ashe as the Winkie Guard.

Whether my personal enthusiasm for this project had inspired my team and colleagues in some manner, or just through sheer serendipity, this tribute turned into quite a magnificent affair. The first character who people got to see was the Winkie Guard, who, complete with tall hat and staff, was an imposing 7' 6" green monster stationed in front of the entrance to the event. Jerry Maren, one of only 14 living actors who played Munchkin characters in the film 60 years earlier, sang, danced, and told off-color *Oz* makeup jokes, bringing the house down. As always, I showed video slides and footage, providing a brief back-

119

drop to the *Oz* legend, utilizing my research materials, and calling up special guests. Rob Burman, another industry artist (and husband of Jennifer, our Winkie Guard costume designer), created beautiful plaques which we gave to Maren and the living descendants of others who had worked on the original film. I was personally thrilled when Charles Schram, who did the Cowardly Lion's makeup in the original *Oz* film but was unable to attend the tribute, sent me a letter of thanks for including him in the proceedings. But the true highlight of the event was the characters themselves. Corso and his team, including Kenny and Karen Myers (whose Cinémakeup Studios was our *Oz* makeup central), Kevin Haney, who had won an Academy Award for *Driving Miss Daisy*, Ve Neill, who had won three Oscars and been nominated for several others, and artists Richard Snell and Deborah Patino, did an amazing job of re-creating the original 1939 looks. All of the actors played their parts using dialogue and song lyrics that I had written for them, based on similar words from the original film screenplay and songs. No cast members or makeup people received any money from this event; everyone came together to honor a legendary Hollywood picture. For me, it was the chance of a lifetime – here was a major Hollywood anniversary, and I was the *only* one in town who had conceived and created a major tribute to mark the occasion. I had learned to wear whatever hat was required for the project, and my *Oz* affair took my writing and independent producing ventures to the next level.

Before guests entered the tribute to *The Wizard of Oz*, they were greeted by the imposing figure of the Winkie Guard, with makeup by Todd Tucker (pictured with performer Rob Ashe) and costume by Jennifer McManus.

120

Rob Burman created these honorary plaques for people attached to the original *Oz* legend.

Charles Schram, who did makeup for the original 1939 *Oz* movie, sent this letter to the author after he received his plaque.

Dear Scott,

      I wish to thank you for your part in giving me the very beautiful plaque of the Wizard of Oz characters. When you are 87 years old and people remember some work that you had done 60 years ago, it is a very nice feeling indeed. Thank you again.

Sincerely,

Chas. H. Schram

Early in my conception of the *Oz* tribute, I learned that Warner Bros. was planning to re-release a refurbished version of the 1939 film for Christmas of 1998. And though I had been eagerly corresponding with the chief publicist of the re-release, they eventually backed out of involvement in my project. However, as several Warner Bros. craftspeople were at my tribute, including the chief of their makeup department, I knew that word would eventually get back to them about what we had achieved. Three weeks later, I was called in by my original contact in Warner Bros.' publicity department, and I could see his wheels start turning when he viewed some of my rough tribute footage. Between the two of us, we devised a plan to bring five of our

121

characters to Warner Bros.' grand opening of the film, a world press screening at Mann's Chinese Theater in Hollywood on Halloween morning. We arranged to have the makeups done at the historic Warner Bros. makeup department, then transport the characters to the Chinese Theater in a limousine. What we didn't know was that 3000 people would be waiting at the theater at 9AM to see us. All of the characters were greeted with near hysteria by the adoring crowd — mostly a sea of parents with *Oz* character-clad children — and entertained dozens of members from the press. As a result, several of the performers were featured on the evening news in interview segments, giving speeches, and mingling with the audience on the "Walk of Fame" in front of the theater. Using her marvelous improvisational comic skills, Denise Moses, who played our Wicked Witch, traded barbs with newscasters and wound up on several wraparound nightly news segments.

Denise Moses had portrayed the Wicked Witch in an Energizer Bunny TV commercial and joined the author at both his original tribute and again at the Mann's Chinese Theater appearance on Halloween of 1998. With her uncanny resemblance to Margaret Hamilton's original Wicked Witch and brilliant comic skills, Moses was a hit with the press and fans alike.

It was truly a magical moment, and realize this: it all evolved out of writing about makeup artistry. Without my initial writing work, none of the rest of it would have fallen into place. In fact, after the Chinese Theater appearance, I wrote an extensive article about the history of *The Wizard of Oz* and its makeup achievements - truly a benchmark in cinema history - for Makeup Artist Magazine, a sui generis writing experience that became the lead story in a magazine, and one of the prominent focal points in the industry in the fall of 1998. *Oz* was a hot topic, and though the re-release fell short of expectations, I would like to think that my efforts, at least in part, helped bring the story into public view during that time. It was an exciting moment and a true industry achievement. And, of course, I made my finest video documentary about the entire experience - with music, footage, the makeup process, guest speakers, the works.

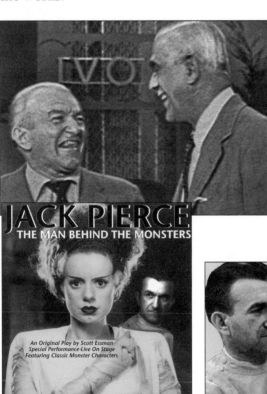

For the author's next project, he is planning to stage the life of Jack Pierce, the make-up artist who created the original *Frankenstein* monster and many other classic horror characters. Here, Pierce is pictured honoring Boris Karloff on a 1957 episode of *This is Your Life*. Also pictured is Pierce transforming Karloff into the monster for *Frankenstein* in 1931.

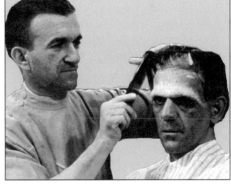

Future Projects

Is there an end or a limit to my special events? The answer to that question is given throughout this book: so long as I continue to be a freelance writer in Hollywood, I plan to immerse myself and develop innovative projects about the worlds I am covering. Certainly, I plan to take the events in different directions. For one, I will stage the life work of Jack Pierce, the legendary makeup pioneer who created the original monsters for Universal Studios classics including *Frankenstein, The Mummy, The Bride of Frankenstein, The Wolf Man* and *Phantom of the Opera*. More a special event than a tribute, the Pierce project, once again with special makeup character re-creations, will first be performed live in Pasadena during June of 2000. For the event, I enlisted the help of Rob Burman and Jennifer McManus, who each worked on my *Wizard of Oz* tribute. With Rob supervising makeup and Jennifer designing costumes, the Pierce event is sure to be a visual delight. Beyond that, I may attempt to take Pierce's life into the docu-drama film arena. Based on my intensive research about the man, I have written a full-length screenplay. While too difficult and inclusive to present it on stage as written, I am planning to fashion it as a narrative Hollywood biopic for the screen. In October of 1999, I published an in-depth article in <u>Makeup Artist Magazine</u> about Pierce's work, and I am planning to write a detailed biography about his career. Going from special live events to books and feature films is a stretch, but I have methodically built on my previous successes and plan to continue to strategically expand them into whatever direction is most logical, challenging, and fresh.

For the author's next planned project, a live stage show celebrating the work of makeup artist Jack Pierce, he enlisted the services of the husband-and-wife team of Rob Burman and Jennifer McManus, whose STICKS AND STONES studio worked on the author's tribute to *The Wizard of Oz*. Pictured here are Burman and McManus with the costumes that they designed and created for the movie *Mighty Morphin' Power Rangers*.

If any ideas in this chapter stir you into wanting to expand your own concept of journalism, just realize that each of my events started with a simply idea, then gradually built up until I had the support of many talented people. You can take a freelance writing career in many exciting areas. Granted, you never want to spread yourself too thin, as writing will likely always be your metier — it is certainly still mine — but trying to create special projects can invigorate your career. Even if you stay with the written word, there are inventive projects that you can undertake on your own: the road to self-publishing is a path that you can surely and safely pursue. As I will describe in Chapter 9, with the advent of desktop publishing, creating original written projects is a potent way for freelance writers to gain total control of their writing destinies.

Chapter Nine

SELF-PUBLISHING

As we have entered the era of self-contained multi-media home computer systems, one viable outlet for freelance writers who desire greater command of their work is to self-publish. While this is not always recommended, freelance writers certainly hold the option on publishing their own material should they run aground in trying to place their writing with a mainstream publication. Of course, your life is much easier as a freelancer if you have established venues for your work: you have a guaranteed audience, you have a built-in understanding of the market for various types of stories, and your efforts are typically limited to simply submitting the written piece itself. When you self-publish any type of written material, you must prepare yourself for a great deal of organizational and creative effort. Often, self-publishing involves all the stages of writing, plus formatting, proofing, printing, marketing, and distribution. While the downside is budgeting enough time, money, and energy for the entire publishing process, you will enjoy greater control of your material and not be at the mercy of another editor or publisher's ultimate decisions about your work.

The Tools

Three things are necessary to self-publish, assuming that you have no true support system outside of immediate friends and contacts. First, you must have an adequate word processing program (usually a given if you have already established a freelance career). Microsoft Word seems to have taken control of the market as of this printing, with the proliferation of their Office program at schools, in pre-packaged software bundles, and on most desktop systems. ClarisWorks (now called AppleWorks) is a fine system that also comes with some desktops and is more user-friendly in some ways than Word (which often assumes too much about writing preferences for my tastes). WordPerfect used to be my WP of choice, but it seems to be relegated to IBM-compatible systems, which I will get to in the hardware section below.

Secondly, and more of a stretch for many writers, is acquiring functional knowledge of a photo digitization and manipulation program, an aspect of desktop publishing monopolized by Adobe PhotoShop. As you will discover during your interactions with publications for whom you regularly contribute material, photos are the lifeblood of printing. Often, I have been told by publishers (even those who have the utmost respect for the writing process) that a great story idea I have pitched is un-publishable unless there is accompanying "art," or photo material. Thus, if your self-publishing ventures are to be complete, you *must* gain at least baseline knowledge of PhotoShop. While there are other programs available, even Hollywood experts have told me that PhotoShop is still the best image manipulation program ever written. With the variety of layer and filter effects PhotoShop offers, a self-publisher can input photoimagery from negatives, photo prints and slides, then select, crop, retouch, colorize, and superimpose any desired images for eventual assembly into his publication. Due to the inherent power of PhotoShop, a basic understanding of the dynamics involved in scanning, resizing, compositing, brightening and color balancing a photograph is essential to creating documentation which includes photo material. As of this printing, PhotoShop has released a Version Five, ostensibly with new tools and capabilities. I have used Version Four for the past several years, and it manages to do the job rather well. Most of my training has been hands-on, but there are recommended books and classes which will orient you to the basics of the program (try the Adobe website for a quick introduction). Once you are familiar enough with PhotoShop (or, perhaps, a useful competing program), you will be able to borrow photos from your subjects, scan them in, and manipulate them for your uses. Once you have saved the photos on your permanent storage hardware, you can return borrowed photos but still have the use of the digital versions for as long as you wish. And so long as your storage devices stay intact, the quality of digital imagery never decreases! If you are confident in your word

128

processing and photo manipulation skills, you are ready for the home publishing phase of creating your own publications.

Lastly in the process, one must gain basic knowledge of a desktop publishing program. This type of software simply allows you to create documents that integrate text, photographs and graphics, and makes it easy to manipulate these items in any manner you choose on a page-by-page basis. Essentially, you create various sized boxes in which you can insert previously written text, logos, photos (or the desired parts of photos) and other elements. While published work in the past was produced through laborious paste-ups and layouts, publishing programs now allow you to integrate all of your elements on your computer, changing styles, formats and layouts with the click of a mouse until you are satisfied. It would be unthinkable to create original documents without these programs, and if you intend to self-publish, a rudimentary knowledge of any home publishing program is mandatory. For many years, Adobe PageMaker was king of this market and it is still a fine program. However, the industry standard among the many printers and magazines I have researched is QuarkXPress. Adaptable to both Macintosh and IBM platforms, Quark allows a user to fluidly create and manipulate documents. Refined versions of the program regularly update Quark's diverse features. Basically, shifting the position and scaling the relative sizes of the boxes is where Quark truly lets you become the master of your publication. In one 18-week Quark class (and much subsequent practice), I have gained a decent level of competence on the program, and though I have much to learn, I feel capable of creating fairly polished documents and publications at this point. As I could not afford a graphic designer for most of my endeavors, it was **vital** that I learned Quark (or a similar application) when I finally chose to self-publish my material.

129

The Hardware

I must warn you that there is bias in this section: I am a Macintosh person through and through. Though I appreciate the power of the IBM compatible systems, I have also witnessed their rigidity. Macs allow for easy access to multiple programs, are exceptionally user friendly, and give writers the freedom to work simultaneously with word processing, photo manipulation, and desktop publishing. Listing a preferred system in this paragraph almost seems pointless – by the time you have this book in hand, there will have been three upgrades from the current popular models! In general, you need a sufficient amount of hard drive storage to create desktop publishing documents. I would recommend at minimum acquiring a 3-gigabyte hard drive, 64 megabytes of RAM, and a 100-MB Zip Drive. These specs are on the low side, considering the amount of memory now available on home systems, but unless you are publishing a 100-page color catalogue with dozens of 8 1/2" x 11" photographs, you will not *need* more than the aforementioned amounts of storage space. For maximum flexibility, I would recommend a Power PC Macintosh desktop system, and note my reasoning: these systems can read **both** Macintosh and IBM-compatible floppy/ZIP disks/CDs, but most IBM machines can **not** read similar information on Mac disks. If you are actively exchanging stored material with your subjects, contributing writers, printing houses, or using any external computers, you are going to be thankful for such adaptability.

As of this writing, you can expect to spend about $2500 on a complete Mac system as described above, once you have purchased a keyboard, monitor, and decent quality scanner (which can provide you with at least 300 dots-per-inch of photo resolution). Scanning software such as VistaScan easily interfaces with PhotoShop, giving you the power to import photos for immediate manipulation on your desktop. Typically, photo quality can vary from monitor to monitor and from system to system, so you may need to put in extra hours in front of your printing house's workstation to check that your photos are properly color balanced and brightened. As far as physically printing your material at home, consider all of your printouts test versions for your ultimate document. As such, you will not require a pricey printer at home – anything that is reasonably priced won't do an optimal job of creating finished printed work, so unless you are independently wealthy, settle for a basic $150 tabletop version that can print letters, envelopes, and simple documents. Prior to running your final job, printing houses will gladly (and likely free of charge) print out your entire document on their standard 1-color (printer code for "black ink") laser printer for your examination, and high-resolution color ink jet printouts allow you to see a test version of the final job, albeit at a substantial cost. What you may wish to wait for is a complete test printing of the final version of the document as it will appear on the actual printing press. Called "blue-lines," these blue-tinted pages will offer you a close rendition of your job as it will appear in the final printed version. If you are printing any pages in color, either a full 4-color process or with one additional color to black, you will likely want a "match print" of the material so that you can carefully examine the ultimate clarity and color balance of the elements in your job in a high-quality glossy printout.

If you are in fact creating huge documents, your photo and publishing files are going to take up undue amounts of memory, and then it will be necessary to upgrade. In this case, buying a CD burner and possibly a JAZ drive may be necessary. Though blank CDs can hold 650 MB of memory and only cost $2-$3 per CD, the burners are typically in the $300-$400 range and up (comparatively, ZIP drives are usually in the $125 range and ZIP disks cost about $10 per disk in bulk; JAZ drives and disks, which hold 1 gigabyte of information, are respectively even more expensive). During the development of this book, I found out that 2-gigabyte storage now exists on new types of disks. There seems to be no end to the limits of data storage that users want, and the costs seem to increase accordingly. Faster and more potent equipment is always being manufactured; very little of this, however, is commensurate with the immediate financial rewards of most writing projects. Still, any computer system is an investment and will pay off as you engage in more complicated self-published works.

Despite the cost and intricacies involved, having a complete desktop system is essential for any writer who wishes to expand into self-publishing. Five years ago, I resisted the idea of having a home computer system — for me, a word processor was enough — but now I swear by my system. Computers are not nearly as challenging as they might seem to an outsider — I find a great deal of my learning is done in a hands-on situation. My recommendation is a one-semester adult education class in Word, Quark, and PhotoShop at a college or university which is equipped with technology applicable to what you might use at home. From there, graduate to a system similar to the one I outlined, and you'll be glad you made the leap. It will allow you to do the work previously dominated by a horde of expensive middlemen in the publication process. With enough sharpening of your desktop skills, as you complete a document to your satisfaction, you will be able to walk right into a print shop with everything on a disk or CD. The printers will be able to go directly to paper from there. This is already a reality, and the procedure of taking a document to its final printed version will only continue to become simplified for independent desktop publishers.

One last word about computers of all extractions: **Back up all of your files on a regular basis!** You never know when a hard drive is going to crash, a virus is going to infect a disk, or Internet caches are going to clog your RAM. Believe me when I tell you that you don't want to learn the hard way to always have everything on your desktop backed up onto ZIP, CD, JAZ or other removable media. This book, in fact, was nearly lost when I encountered a hard drive malfunction. Should this happen to you, the hassle of going to a "data recovery specialist" is looming in your future. That is, unless you can afford to lose all of your files.

Among the author's self-published works is an independently produced industry magazine, DIRECTED BY: The Cinema Quarterly, a periodical devoted to the study of motion-picture directors and their craft.

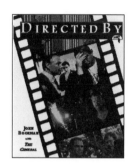

Finding a Market

If you have read this far into Chapter 9, you must have an innate desire to self-publish your own work. In my case, having written for half a dozen different magazines in my years working as a freelancer, I decided to launch my own periodical. Noting their various successes and shortcomings, I engaged a friend, Carsten Dau, who had similar interests in film and film craft, and created Directed By: The Cinema Quarterly, a periodical that would cover the art and craft of cinema directors in a critical forum. While other magazines had certainly featured directors in articles and interviews, with the exception of the Directors Guild of America magazine, no publication was fully devoted to film analysis and retrospectives strictly from the director's point of view. With that in mind, and with my basic knowledge of desktop publishing, I turned an early-1990s dream into a reality in 1997, when we recruited a subject for our first planned issue.

Director Bryan Singer was a friend of mine from USC who had broken through the film festival scene to enormous mainstream success with *The Usual Suspects*, an independently-produced film that went on to win two Academy Awards. Though I had been out of touch with Singer in the intervening years since film school, he granted us a feature story interview about his follow-up to *Suspects*, a moody Stephen King adaptation called *Apt Pupil*. During this in-depth interview, we deconstructed Singer's work, covering all of his projects, his artistic preferences, and his working methods. After attending an early preview screening of *Apt Pupil*, I conducted a follow-up interview with Singer in which I specifically targeted the making of that film. With all of the key feature article information about Singer intact and several personal associates contributing supplementary articles, we started to format and prepare the first issue of <u>Directed By</u>.

Though only 500 copies of that first issue were printed, it was a $4000 investment including self-publishing materials, the cost of printing a 4-color cover, and using high-quality paper, all elements that we felt were necessary to properly launch a serious magazine about cinema. But this was money well spent, as we were able to attract significant attention from key figures in Singer's team, Phoenix Pictures, who released *Apt Pupil*, and magazine retailers and distributors in the Hollywood area. Self-publishing on this scale is an important step in taking a freelance career to a higher level; as such, the funds required to get <u>Directed By</u> off the ground were budgeted as a long-term proposition with little compensation expected in return during the near future.

In self-publishing a new magazine, one immediate problem built into the system is the catch-22 of acquiring distribution. Regardless of the quality of your publication, you are going to be caught between big distributors who want a guaranteed size and circulation before they pick you up and small distributors who do not have the circulation power to get your work to a wide range of outlets. For the first <u>Directed By</u>, we were forced to self-distribute, which basically meant driving from bookstore to newsstand, handing out magazines from boxes in my hatchback. However, due to the quality of our product (untold hours spent writing and re-writing our articles, and days on end spent perfecting the format as much as we could), we were able to acquire wide newsstand and specialty bookstore distribution in the Los Angeles, New York, and Seattle areas for our second issue (which featured the career of John Boorman). Utilizing other aspects of the writing process as described throughout this book, I was soon able to capital-ize on our <u>Directed By</u> achievements by gaining the trust and participation of other directors including John Sayles, Kevin Smith, and Ron Shelton. Building on the strengths of the first two issues, we accumulated a variety of other resources, including talented graphic artists, contributing writers, and a base of publicists who offer us new projects for coverage. As of this printing, <u>Directed By</u> issue #3 will have an even wider distribution and feature three directors from the inventive HBO TV series *The Sopranos*. Our intention is to progressively improve the quality and distribution of the magazine, hopefully arriving at a national book outlet or prominent sponsor in the near future so that we will be able to support our production costs. Similar to my other freelance endeavors, <u>Directed By</u> is the product of my personal interests, writing experiences, and desire to form my own niche within the Hollywood media. At this point, even though we are still a fledgling operation, we have parlayed an idea into a legitimate industry publication which has the respect of both the feature film directing community and Hollywood circles at large. As far as creating original self-published works, when content, advertising, and distribution are all working harmoniously, a publication will surely flourish, but you must give it time and attention.

For the third issue of the author's self-published magazine, <u>Directed By: The Cinema Quarterly</u>, three directors of HBO's successful series *The Sopranos* will be profiled.

E-Publications

Without a doubt, Internet-based sites are the future of desktop publishing. Even now, potential outlets for freelance writers are cropping up on a daily basis. If you latch onto such a site, your work will get exposure in an up and coming forum and you are sure to make further connections and reach new audiences. If you are especially industrious, beginning your own website is another alternative. For relatively little expense (especially compared to the costs of printing a magazine of any substance), one can claim a domain name on the World Wide Web and begin to publish original material on a regular basis. While the Internet has been overrun by such sites of late, do not discount their value – the web is an important promotional tool for any media project, and it would not surprise me if it seriously challenges (if not entirely eliminates) similarly-themed print publications within the next decade. Think of the simple math: printing in the 4-color CMYK process is very expensive – it can cost you hundreds of dollars per page on a basic run of 1000 magazines. It costs **nothing** extra to publish color photos on the web, and except for memory limitations, you are free to post as many pictures as you desire. With regards to memory, where a 300-dpi color 8" x 10" photo might require at least 10 MB of memory, the standard web resolution of 72 dpi and satisfactory 3" x 5" size of that same photo might only require 300K of memory. To create attractive web sites, many software programs, including PageMill and FrontPage, circumvent the need to learn HTML or other web programming languages and can be easily utilized by the basic computer user. If you already possess the skills required for self-published documents, translating your material to the Internet will be a logical and simple undertaking for you.

After I engaged in a basic e-mail relationship with Todd Vaziri, the proprietor of *Visual Effects Headquarters*, www.vfxhq.com, a website devoted to special visual effects in films, TV shows and media projects, I was asked to contribute material, leading to three published articles on their site. Not only did the site get thousands of "hits" per week, my profiles of stop-motion animators and creature creators were so well received, other offers to write for various websites arrived in my e-mailbox on a regular basis. Though vfxhq is now defunct, I credit them with showcasing my writing to an international audience, specifically facilitating my ongoing relationship with L'Ecran

<u>Fantastique</u>, a French magazine for whom I became the "official U.S. correspondent" following their first exposure to my work on vfxhq.

Currently, I write for an online film, culture, music and arts site, *Nuvein Online*, having created a special monthly column called "CinNews" in which I profile cinema artists. I have also written music reviews and retrospectives for *Nuvein,* and with the help of proprietor Enrique Diaz and his staff, we have developed websites for <u>Directed By</u> and my special June, 2000 event about makeup legend Jack Pierce. On an ongoing basis, I will make sure to devote the proper resources to keep my projects on the web at all times. Consider that the Internet as we now know it is truly in its infancy. In 1995, for example, it was little more than a list of topic-based newsgroups. While it was an interesting center for written communications even at that time, its expansion over the past five years has been astounding. As the web will surely have a long and varied life while its potential is explored, on-line resources are unquestionably the most potent future outlets for writers of all extractions.

Among the author's best memories as a freelance writer are (from left), lecturing at the SHOWBIZ EXPO, covering Disney's remake of *Mighty Joe Young*, and creating a multi-media project about makeup artistry, *CREATURE PEOPLE*.

138

Chapter Ten

YOUR WRITING FUTURE

To reiterate a concept that I introduced very early in these pages, your writing career will be what you make of it. Since becoming a freelancer is such an unstructured process, the door is wide open for you to make informed choices and steer your career into fruitful directions. For me, writing about makeup artistry was a ticket to covering Hollywood, but that choice was not the only one available to me. And though I produced several original makeup-oriented projects to help me assimilate into Hollywood, my subjects could have just as well have been soap opera directors, heavy metal singers, or pro hockey players. Writing about a specific strand of entertainment is ultimately an individual choice; the key is tapping into a field which has *not* already been overexposed in print and electronic media. Originality might be your best ticket to success — it is paramount that you select a subject for which you have an angle that has not been successfully exploited to date. Makeup artistry was a subject in which I had a great deal of personal interest in makeup artistry; I enjoyed researching its history, interviewing its key craftspeople, and learning about various techniques and projects in the field. It is vital that you have a similar strong interest in your chosen specialty if you are going to infuse your writing with enough passion to convince Hollywood that you're a worthy contributor to its media machine.

In sculpting a freelance career, here are some additional pointers that might spare you the growing pains that the uninitiated are often forced to endure:

• **Pick them before they pick you.**

After they acquire a reputation for being reliable, knowledgeable contributors to a particular subject, freelance writers are often tapped by publications to cover specific types of stories (in this instance pigeonholing is not necessarily a bad thing). However, you should be one step ahead of the process in this sense, continually finding your *own* story ideas and subjects to cover and pitching those concepts to the publications yourself. The world meets no one halfway—particularly not in Hollywood—and you don't want to rely on "them" to call you with assignments when you're trying to maintain a steady income in the freelance world.

• **Always settle your financial situation up front.**

In my experience, writers can be paid as little as $50 for a 500-word article and as much as $3000 for an article over 10,000 words. If you expect a certain amount for a written work (whether assigned or initiated from one of your pitches), don't be fearful of establishing your needs with the publisher before you start. While some publications work with written contracts or memos, many rely on "verbal" agreements. Be careful of this, unless you have already formed a good relationship with the publisher and do not require a written contract. If you value your long-term future with a magazine, bickering about money will not serve your interests—remember that you do not "work" for a company per se; you are essentially an independent contractor. However, there is *nothing* wrong with firmly establishing financial guidelines. Get an approximate word count for your assignment and arrange payment accordingly (if it isn't already fixed– for instance, a standard rate of 10-20 cents per word). Anticipate the requirements for completing the assignment – how many interviews will it take? Will you transcribe them yourself, or will you have to pay to have someone transcribe them? Also, how intricate is the assignment in terms of research, fact-checking, acquiring technical background information? All of these factors should enter the negotiation for payment for a written assignment. If you have side projects that would benefit from the exposure of being featured in an industry magazine, bartering for advertising space is the best way to make use of your work with a publication, especially if they are willing to offer you the pricey space in lieu of what would have been a moderate amount of pay for your written work.

• Build and call upon your key industry connections.

If your work has spoken to your abilities and commitment as a writer, your reputation should be well established with your subjects. Since Hollywood is a town built on reputations and perceptions, this can only help your career in several ways. First, your contacts will want to work with you! This is vitally important in an industry where your professional associates are frequently the ones who refer you to new jobs and developing projects. Whether you have work that requires the contribution of others — a writing assignment that needs quotes from Hollywood luminaries — or they have work that they send to you, your connections will irrevocably play an ongoing role in your working life. They certainly did so in my career.

• Be careful of accepting staff writing positions.

This might sound like counterproductive advice; after all, isn't the goal of all freelance writers to eventually work on the staff of a magazine, newspaper or other periodical? Yes and no. Becoming a staff writer can have definite advantages: full-time regular work, salary, possible benefits packages, etc. However, the freedoms that you enjoy (in all senses) as a freelance writer soon evaporate when you take a staff position. While being independent typically means that you have an array of choices and can selectively accept writing assignments as your interest and schedule permits, being on staff at a publication translates into doing work that you are handed, with an editor or senior writer determining the assignments. As in any office, you may find yourself within a political atmosphere that contains hidden pitfalls. In brief, my advice is not to dismiss staff positions, but carefully examine the working atmosphere at the publication you are considering. Will the editor be someone who listens to your needs? Are there ingrown politics with other staff writers that may affect your career there? Will you be happy regardless of the assignments you get? Use extreme caution!

• Diversify as much as possible.

Earlier, I discussed pigeonholing, which can be a benefit if you are struggling to find *any* kind of writing work; in this instance, you want Hollywood insiders to think that *you* are the person to call on to write about a specific subject. Yet as soon as it is feasible, begin to stretch your wings. Don't be afraid to go into untested waters, expanding into new subject areas, working with new publications, and developing unique projects. Every year throughout my career, I have methodically introduced a fresh element into my coterie of freelance projects: approaching a new publication, interviewing a new type of Hollywood artist, or developing a new special project that will further my career. You don't need to wait ten years before you start to expand. Constant change is the one permanent aspect of building a freelance career, and you must embrace the change and maintain as much flexibility as you can. As soon as you are comfortable with your position as a freelancer and detect that there are other facets of the Hollywood machine for you to explore, go forward with your strongest ideas and take the necessary steps to have them taken seriously.

I leave you with a final thought: the more that you rely on your dreams to guide you through the process of gaining a foothold as a freelancer, the more apt you are to succeed. After all, this is Hollywood, land of dreams. Approach the possibilities of a freelance career with as much hope and anticipation as you can muster. Perhaps one day you will find yourself in the middle of a big Hollywood movie set, hanging out with the director, producer, cast, crew... maybe even interacting with a fantasy character whom you loved in your childhood. For a frustrated screenwriter from the LA suburbs with no money, no connections, and no resources, I found myself in exactly that position within five years. Now I honestly want to see it happen to you. And if you are able to utilize the concepts herein proactively, be sure to let me know about it! Here's one last item I will share with you, hoping to leave you with a final dose of inspiration before you set off into Hollywood:

LAST NIGHT IN WHOVILLE
Article by Scott Essman

Note: An excerpt of this piece was first published in –

"Twas the night before Grinchmas, and all through Stage 16, not a makeup character was stirring, not even mean green!" - S.E.

After five months of principal photography at Universal Studios, Hollywood, and many more weeks of tests and preparation, the biggest makeup film in modern Hollywood history wound down on Tuesday, January 11, 2000. Though *THE GRINCH* will continue to shoot on location, with pick-ups, second-unit photography, and re-shoots scheduled through February and likely into the spring, January 11 represented the last day of big calls that has made this production unprecedented in the makeup community. Also, one location trip to Utah in late March is still remaining on the schedule, reportedly for a scene familiar to fans of the story in which the dastardly Grinch rushes down a tremendous snowy slope in a Santa Claus-like sled, eager to invade Whoville.

Due to be released in November of 2000, *THE GRINCH* is a live-action version of Dr. Seuss' familiar Christmas tale, "How The Grinch Stole Christmas," originally written in 1957 as a poem, then a book, then presented as a treasured animated short in 1966. As directed by Ron Howard, this *GRINCH* stars Jim Carrey as the green guy who steals everyone's favorite holiday from a town full of Whos. In a landmark concept that eclipses such makeup-intensive classics as *PLANET OF THE APES* and *THE WIZARD OF OZ*, every character onscreen in *THE GRINCH* wears a prosthetic-based makeup, designed and created by Rick Baker's Cinovation studio. Other visual effects and digital enhancements are being provided by Digital Domain.

143

While Carrey's character makeup is regularly applied by Kazuhiro Tsuji in a special trailer with direct access to the secretive set, many of the other characters are made up and costumed on the cavernous Stage 16, a soundstage which has been completely converted into *GRINCH* makeup central. The Imagine-Universal co-production also stars Jeffrey Tambor, Molly Shannon, Christine Baranski and Bill Erwin as principal

Jim Carrey forecasting his Grinch role on the set of his Andy Kaufman biopic, *Man on the Moon*.

The new *GRINCH* is based on the 1957 Dr. Seuss story which was first filmed as an animated featurette in 1966.

Whos, with makeups by Kevin Haney, Kenny Myers, Ve Neill, and Bill Corso, respectively. Toni G has undertaken the enormous task of heading-up Baker's makeup department, which has often featured as many as 40 makeup artists in addition to the numerous hairstylists, costumers, and support personnel required to create the many Whos. January 11 was goodbye for most of the makeup crew, a majority of whom were on the show from early September, 1999. Baker and Toni G bade farewell to their makeup artists, citing their dedication, consistency, and superb craftsmanship through the long but reportedly rewarding production. "At first, I wasn't sure about turning so many makeups over to other artists," Baker told his huge makeup team before they left to supervise a final exterior night shoot, "but I soon realized that you guys were all doing great work and that I had very few creative problems to worry about." This achievement is all the more remarkable considering that Baker is simultaneously supervising the makeup for *NUTTY PROFESSOR 2*. In that project,

144

David LeRoy Anderson is applying all of Eddie Murphy's makeups on a daily basis for a sequel to the film which brought both he and Baker Academy Awards three years ago.

Most strikingly, the outdoor set for the film is astounding: first of all, it is nestled atop the large Universal Studios hill that overlooks their primary backlot. On one side of the set, the legendary house from 1960's *PSYCHO* sits, and on the other side, one can find the house from the remade version of the same movie from 1998. In back of The *GRINCH* set, sitting in a darkened moat like a monster itself is the control bunker from the climactic ending of *THE LOST WORLD*. If that weren't enough, the main *GRINCH* set itself might outdo them all: with surreal production design by Michael Corenblith, the central town of Whoville stands high among the other Universal monuments. Houses, vehicles, and special props (like the musical instruments in the mayor's private marching band) offer a combination of innovation in live-action filmmaking with a definite homage to Dr. Seuss' original designs. Multi-colored Christmas decorations and lights dance on and off around the set, which is completely surrounded by an artificial hill blanketed with tall trees. Snow, in this case made with small shreds of paper and lightly colored sand, cover the Who homes and streets. To the naked eye, Corenblith and his crew have captured the spirit of the original *Grinch* film, with sets that perfectly match the concepts of Baker's makeups and Rita Ryack's delightful costumes.

On this night, the only mystery remains The Grinch himself. As played by Jim Carrey, this Grinch is animal in nature, with hairy hands and arms, and an upright tuft of green locks upon his head. The mask of his face which sits in Stage 16 is quite remarkable, suggesting the character from the 1966 cartoon while retaining its own unique visual qualities. Carrey's appearance will likely be a combination of a modeled character mask and a complete facial makeup, and by all accounts, his character will not be the only Grinch creature in the film – a smaller version seems evident as well! Nonetheless, no one gets in to see the actual Grinch in his makeup and costume except the closest cast and crew members, and security (and Carrey as well) have been very careful about allowing any visitors to see him before the movie is released.

With all of the attention to visual detail apparent in the production, it goes without saying that this *GRINCH* will be one of the true prizes in fantasy films for this year, and given its Christmastime distribution date, it will be sure to stir the imaginations of its audiences.

Jim Carrey as the title character in Ron Howard's *THE GRINCH*, due in theaters in 2000. Through the contacts he had made in Hollywood since his first endeavors as a freelance writer five years ago, the author was invited to the set on the last major day of principal photography to meet the cast and crew.

With this publication, I have reached the end of one road and hope to start another to coincide with the arrival of our new century. We all reach different plateaus in our writing careers, and this book represents the culmination of one of those for me. I eagerly await the next phase of the journey from this point forward.

Scott Essman

Universal City
100 Universal City Plaza
Universal City, CA. 91608

STILL NEED DIRECTION? HELP IS AVAILABLE!

The author's newly established
FREELANCE WRITERS ASSOCIATION
offers consultation to aspiring and professional writers in all fields.

Charter members include authors and contributing writers from magazines mentioned in this book, including <u>Directed By: The Cinema Quarterly</u>, <u>Makeup Artist Magazine</u>, <u>MovieMaker</u>, <u>Creative Screenwriting</u>, and *Nuvein Online*.

The FWA is designed to assist writers in creative and technical matters that arise in trying to develop, pitch, research, write, and market original written material geared for publication.

To find out more about how to join the FWA on a trial basis, send an e-mail or letter with SASE to the author:

Scott Essman
P.O. Box 1722
Glendora, CA 91740

scottessman@yahoo.com

The FWA is a media organization under the jurisdiction of
VISIONARY MEDIA © 2000, Scott Essman.

Script Magic
Subconscious Techniques to Conquer Writer's Block

Marisa D'Vari

Script Magic answers the prayers of every screenwriter who's ever spent time staring down a blank page. Pursuing the dream of landing that big script sale can be stressful, and that stress and pressure can be counter-productive to the writing process. *Script Magic* is a powerful antidote to writer's block that both professional and aspiring creative writers can benefit from, based on a deceptively simple principle: If you're not having fun writing it, your script probably isn't going to be any fun to read, either. And if it's not fun to read, how is it ever going to be sold and made into a movie that people will want to spend their money to see?

Using easy and fun techniques designed to circumvent the practical, critical conscious mind and tap into the rich creative resources of the subconscious mind, readers will learn how to revitalize their writing and improve their productivity. Create engaging characters, dialogue that jumps off the page and screenplays that sell!

MARISA D'VARI has 20 years of hands-on experience working in Hollywood as a studio story analyst, consultant and executive. She currently produces and hosts her own nationally syndicated cable TV show, "Scene Here," and conducts seminars on screenwriting all over the country. Visit her Web site at **www.scriptmagic.com**.

Doubleday Stage & Screen Selection

$18.95, ISBN 0-941188-74-4
250 pages, 6 x 9
Order # 47RLS

Screenwriting 101
The Essential Craft of Feature Film Writing

Neill D. Hicks

Hicks, a successful screenwriter whose credits include *Rumble in the Bronx* and *First Strike*, brings the clarity and practical instruction familiar to his UCLA students to screenwriters everywhere. In his refreshingly straightforward style, Hicks tells the beginning screen-writer how the mechanics of Hollywood storytelling work, and how to use those elements to create a script with blockbuster potential without falling into cliches. Also dis-cussed are the practicalities of the business—securing an agent, pitch-ing your script, protecting your work, and other topics essential to building a career in screenwriting.

"Neill Hicks makes complex writing concepts easy to grasp, in a way that only a master teacher could. And he does so while keeping his book one hell of a fun read."
Eric Edson, Screenwriter and Executive Director of the Hollywood Symposium

NEILL HICKS is a professional screenwriter and a senior instructor at the UCLA Extension Writer's Program, where he has been honored with the Outstanding Instructor Award. He has also taught graduate courses on screenwriting at the University of Denver, presented a seminar on Selling to Hollywood at the Denver International Film Festival, and conducts screenwriting workshops throughout the United States, Canada, and Europe. Visit his Web site at **www.screenwriting101.net**.

Movie Entertainment Book Club Selection
Doubleday Stage and Screen Selection

$16.95, ISBN 0-941188-72-8
220 pages, 6 x 9
Order # 41RLS

The Writer's Journey
—2nd Edition
Mythic Structure for Writers

Christopher Vogler

1st Edition - Over 100,000 Sold!

THE WRITER'S JOURNEY
2ND EDITION
MYTHIC STRUCTURE FOR WRITERS

CHRISTOPHER VOGLER

See why this book has become an international best seller, and a true classic. First published in 1992, *The Writer's Journey* explores the powerful relationship between mythology and storytelling in a clear, concise style that's made it required reading for movie executives, screenwriters, scholars, and lovers of pop culture all over the world.

Writers of both fiction and non-fiction will discover a set of useful myth-inspired storytelling paradigms (i.e. *The Hero's Journey*) and step-by-step guidelines to plot and character development. Based on the work of Joseph Campbell, *The Writer's Journey* is a must for writers of all kinds interested in further developing their craft.

The updated and revised 2nd edition provides new insights and observations from Vogler's ongoing work on mythology's influence on stories, movies, and man himself.

> *"This is a book about the stories we write, and perhaps more importantly, the stories we live. It is the most influential work I have yet encountered on the art, nature, and the very purpose of storytelling."*
> **Bruce Joel Rubin**, Screenwriter, *Ghost, Jacob's Ladder*

Book of the Month Club Selection • Writer's Digest Book Club Selection • Movie Entertainment Book Club Selection • Doubleday Stage and Screen Selection

CHRIS VOGLER has been a top Hollywood story consultant and development executive for over 15 years. He has worked on such top grossing feature films as *The Thin Red Line*, *Fight Club*, *The Lion King*, and *Beauty and the Beast*. His international workshops have taken him to Germany, Italy, United Kingdom and Spain, and his literary consulting service Storytech provides in-depth evaluations for professional writers. To learn more, visit his Web site at **www.thewritersjourney.com**.

$22.95, ISBN 0-941188-70-1
300 pages, 6 x 9
Order # 98RLS

Myth & the Movies

Discovering the Mythic Structure of 50 Unforgettable Films

Stuart Voytilla

Foreword by **CHRISTOPHER VOGLER**, author of "The Writer's Journey"

With this collection of essays exploring the mythic structure of 50 well-loved U.S. and foreign films, Voytilla has created a fun and fascinating book for film fans, screenwriters, and anyone with a love of storytelling and pop culture.

An informal companion piece to the best-selling *The Writer's Journey* by Christopher Vogler, *Myth and the Movies* applies the mythic structure Vogler developed to films as diverse as "Die Hard," "Singin' in the Rain" and "Boyz N the Hood." This comprehensive book offers a greater understanding of why some films continue to touch and connect with audiences generation after generation.

Movies discussed include *Annie Hall, Beauty and the Beast, Chinatown, Citizen Kane, E.T., The Fugitive, The Godfather, The Graduate, La Strada, The Piano, Pulp Fiction, Notorious, Raiders of the Lost Ark, The Searchers, The Silence of the Lambs, T2–Judgment Day, Sleepless in Seattle, Star Wars, Unforgiven,* and many more.

STUART VOYTILLA is a writer, script consultant, and teacher of acting and screenwriting. He has evaluated hundreds of scripts for LA -based talent agencies. His latest screenplay, *The Golem*, is being produced by Baltimore-based Princess Pictures.

Movie Entertainment Book Club Selection

$26.95, ISBN 0-941188-66-3
300 pages, 7 x 10, illustrations throughout
Order # 39RLS

Writing the Second Act

Building Conflict and Tension in Your Film Script

Michael Halperin, Ph.D.

New! Available Oct. 2000

WRITING THE SECOND ACT

B U I L D I N G

CONFLICT

A N D

TENSION

I N   Y O U R   F I L M   S C R I P T

MICHAEL HALPERIN

Every screenplay needs an attention-grabbing beginning and a satisfying ending, but those elements are nothing without a strong, well-crafted middle. The second act is where most of the action is: where your characters grow, change, and overcome the obstacles that will bring them to the resolution at the end of the story. Naturally, it's also the hardest act to write, and where most screenplays tend to lose momentum and focus. Author Halperin helps you slay the dragon with *Writing the Second Act*, designed especially for helping screenwriters through that crucial 60-page stretch. Structural elements and plot devices are discussed in detail, as well as how to keep the action moving and the characters evolving while keeping the audience completely absorbed in and entertained by your story.

MICHAEL HALPERIN is a professional writer whose numerous credits include TV shows (*Star Trek: The Next Generation, Quincy*), nonfiction books (*Writing Great Characters*), and interactive media programs (*Voyeur*). He has also worked extensively as a consultant in the television industry, including Executive Story Consultant for 20th Century Fox Television and Creative Consultant on the animated series *Masters of the Universe*. He currently teaches screenwriting at Loyola Marymount University in Los Angeles and is in the process of developing a business-to-business Web site for the entertainment industry.

$19.95, ISBN 0-941188-29-9
240 Pages, 6 x 9
Order # 49RLS

Stealing Fire From the Gods

A Dynamic New Story Model for Writers and Filmmakers

James Bonnet

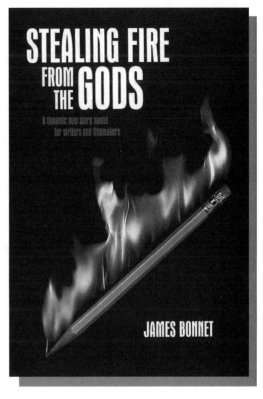

Great stories affect us so much because they teach us about life, and about ourselves. In the tradition of Carl Jung, Joseph Campbell and Christopher Vogler, James Bonnet explores the connection between mythology and personal growth—and the implications that connection has for storytellers in particular.

Unlike films, novels, and other forms of modern storytelling we're accustomed to today, the great myths, legends and fairy tales passed down through the ages were not created by individual authors. They evolved from ancient oral traditions, fueled by forces within the creative unconscious that are still accessible to us today. *Stealing Fire From the Gods* investigates those forces and teaches writers how to use the same elements that make those traditional tales so enduring to make your own stories more powerful, memorable and emotionally resonant. Author James Bonnet takes you on a journey through the creative process of storytelling, uncovering not only what makes a story great but also how the creative process can reconnect us to our lost or forgotten inner selves.

JAMES BONNET, founder of Astoria Filmwrights, is a successful Hollywood screen and television writer. He has acted in or written more than forty television shows and features including *Kojak*, *Barney Miller* and the cult classics *The Blob* and *The Cross and The Switchblade*. Visit his Web site at **www.storymaking.com**.

Movie Entertainment Book Club Selection

$26.95, ISBN: 0-941188-65-5
300 pages, 6 x 9
Order # 38RLS

MICHAEL WIESE PRODUCTIONS

11288 Ventura Blvd., Suite 821
Studio City, CA 91604
1-818-379-8799
kenlee@earthlink.net
www.mwp.com

Write or Fax
for a
free catalog.

Please send me the following
books:

Title   Order Number (#RLS___)   Amount

_____ _____
_____ _____
_____ _____
_____ _____

SHIPPING   _____

California Tax (8.25%)   _____

TOTAL ENCLOSED _____

Please make check or money order payable to
Michael Wiese Productions

(Check one) ____ Master Card ____Visa ____Amex

Credit Card Number_____

Expiration Date_____

Cardholder's Name_____

Cardholder's Signature_____

SHIP TO:

Name_____

Address_____

City_____State_____Zip_____